PRAISE FOR **THE PATIENT ORGANIZATION**

"I was twenty-eight when Walt helped transform my career—and ultimately my life—as we worked together to discover the Seven Questions. His coaching approach through the Seven Questions, his mastery of how those questions tie to Organizational Operating Systems, and his knowledge of how humans work is unmatched. Walt believed in me and gave me the tools to believe even when I may not have believed in myself. I discovered fearlessness, bravery, and Patience on this journey with Walt, and am truly grateful for his friendship."

KERRIE LANG
Millennial Integrator, Thornton Brother Inc.
Athens Ga

"Walt has an incredible ability to connect with his clients in a very simple and authentic manner to get things done. I had run a company for over ten years before first working with Walt, and I wish we had met earlier. In *The Patient Organization*, he has done it again—he's put into words and action the 'lessons learned.' Every organization should be making sure that their people have clear answers to the Seven Questions. This is a book that will produce value when read over and over again. Thanks Walt."

AUSTIN KOON
Davis Moore Capital

"If you aren't running an OOS that answers the Seven Questions, and are just winging it with effort and talent then I truly feel sorry for you. Not because I think you are stupid, but because I have been there before. Can you imagine an NFL team trying to win games or score a touchdown by drawing plays in the dirt? Yet that is exactly how most people choose to run their business. They just make it up as they go along because that is how it has always been. As an organization grows, it needs a system to get to yes on the Seven Questions. It needs core values, it needs a plan and it needs plays it can run on a weekly and daily basis so it can grow. EOS can give your team the complete 7Q playbook. It gives you a system. It teaches you how to run winning plays. So, drop your stick, quit drawing up your business plan in the dirt, and get busy growing in the right direction. Your team and family will thank you."

JAMES CUMMINGS
President, McGreat LLC

"Via the 7Qs, a great OOS, hard work and Walt's help, we have transformed our company. Combined with an effective teaching style, deepseated personal values and leadership training content anchored in the 7Qs, he has helped us convert our leadership team from a group of likable, talented people into a well-armed, well-trained, highly-synchronized group that generates consistent results through an OOS that works. Having an organizational operating system (OOS) has clarified our mission and our operating principles. It has also given our leaders the tools they need to set priorities, objectively measure team members, keep a pulse on elements of the business they cannot see every day, develop effective business strategies and communicate well within and outside their teams. Everything we did is echoed in this book. Patience works."

DAVID HATTER
CEO Arista

"Walt presented the 7Qs to our group on our first retreat and completely transformed our culture with this process. As a founder, I want everyone to have the same passion I have about my business, and with Walt's 7Qs and getting to *yes,* I am now able to develop my staff and have them see their careers within this business while becoming extremely passionate, engaged, and Patient. "

DR. AUSTIN COHEN
Founder, Corrective Chiropractic

"Becoming a Patient Organization is critical to success for any company looking to thrive. It changed the way we think, act and is a major catalyst in our company."

MERCER F STANFIELD
President & COO, Brame

"This is an exciting and much needed contribution from the trenches. Brown has simplified and condensed decades of his pioneering work building Patient Organizations to Seven Questions your team members will answer. This dynamic approach can eliminate dysfunction while achieving significant organizational loyalty and improvement. The results speak for themselves. *Ya gotta' read this book!*"

GREG WALKER
Coach to over three hundred business owners
for more than thirty years

"What I like best about this book is that it's full of what I call 'Waltisms'. As Integrator at Counter Culture, I rely heavily not only on EOS but on the lessons peppered in the EOS coaching from you. I recite them often as 'Waltisms,' nuggets of wisdom or thought provoking questions that help drive an organization's implementation of an OOS.

The Patient Organization compliments EOS well because it helps further define the connection a leader and a company has with the most important (in my opinion) key function of EOS: People. Let's be honest, the EOS tool for the quarterly conversation is conceptual, but this makes it very tangible.

The concept of EATT (evolve, adapt, trust, try) is also really important. It's much more concise than Five Dysfunctions and logically connects trust to actions. It's a powerful reminder of the value and necessity of trust.

Lastly, and man this one kinda' blew my mind—I really like the idea that a company is essentially a fiction, given power by people believing in it. I love it."

BRIAN LUDVIKSEN
Integrator, Counter Culture Coffee

It is impossible to quantify how valuable Walt Brown and his teachings have been to McGreat LLC (dba Great Clips Franchisee) and its owners. There are, of course, the numbers. Since implementing our Organizational Operating System (OOS), EOS, McGreat and its affiliates have expanded our holdings from sixteen to forty-seven Great Clips stores, increased revenues by millions of dollars and even gotten into another franchised concept. Those numbers are easy to recite, but they only tell half the story. The rest of the story is more difficult to quantify because it involves taking the time to understand the value you place on your own emotional health as a business owner—what value would you place on feeling like your business was focused on the right problems, hiring the right people and growing in the right direction? How much would it be worth to you to feel like your business is operating under a set of timeless and repeatable principles that develop your leaders and allow you the freedom and flexibility to enjoy your life on your terms? Quantify the value of those feelings and then, and only then, will you have your answer as to what Walt, the Seven Questions and EOS have meant to McGreat.

JAMES CUMMINGS
President, McGreat LLC

"I LOVED the *The Patient Organization*. It is succinct, laden with insight, and readily applicable. Every entrepreneur should take the Seven Question Survey, it will be transformative for you and your company."

JONATHAN B. SMITH
Author of *Optimize for Growth*

"A fantastic read with philosophical, common sense advice and practical approaches—with tools to inject a high level of employee engagement and a true competitive advantage in your company."

ALEX FREYTAG
Author of *Achieve Your Vision*
Certified EOS Implementer

"Such a deep discovery, these Seven Questions. And I really am impressed with Walt's use of the word Patient ... it's almost the manifestation of self-actualization. Really describes why EOS works."

JILL YOUNG
Honey Badger
Certified EOS Implementer and Author of *Earn It!*
TractionFirst, LLC

"Great insights, wisdom and a lot to learn packed in the copy. It was a bit long for my impatient attention span, but it was chewy and made me think. If you get the Seven Questions, you will get the message. Simple. Walt is a wise man with great insight."

SUE HAWKES
CEO, YESS!
Best-Selling Author
Fellow Honey Badger

"Incredibly insightful and a critical read for anyone wanting to, or struggling with, engaging their employees. The best short book on this topic since *The Great Game of Business* and *Ownership Thinking*."

TOM BOUWER
Author of *What The Heck Is EOS*
International Keynote Speaker
Certified EOS Implementer.

THE
PATIENT
ORGANIZATION

THE
PATIENT
ORGANIZATION

**ATTRACTING, ENGAGING, AND
EMPOWERING TEAM PLAYERS**

WALT BROWN

ForbesBooks

Published by ForbesBooks, Charleston, South Carolina.
Member of Advantage Media Group.

ForbesBooks is a registered trademark, and the ForbesBooks colophon is a trademark of Forbes Media, LLC.

Printed in the United States of America.

10 9 8 7 6 5 4 3 2 1

ISBN: 978-1-94663-3-118
LCCN: 2018941772

Cover and layout design by Melanie Cloth.

This publication is designed to provide accurate and authoritative information in regard to the subject matter covered. It is sold with the understanding that the publisher is not engaged in rendering legal, accounting, or other professional services. If legal advice or other expert assistance is required, the services of a competent professional person should be sought.

Advantage Media Group is proud to be a part of the Tree Neutral® program. Tree Neutral offsets the number of trees consumed in the production and printing of this book by taking proactive steps such as planting trees in direct proportion to the number of trees used to print books. To learn more about Tree Neutral, please visit **www.treeneutral.com**.

Since 1917, the Forbes mission has remained constant. Global Champions of Entrepreneurial Capitalism. ForbesBooks exists to further that aim by bringing the Stories, Passion, and Knowledge of top thought leaders to the forefront. ForbesBooks brings you The Best in Business. To be considered for publication, please visit **www.forbesbooks.com**.

This book is dedicated to my clients and their leadership teams and my millennial friends. Thanks to my wife, Anne, the ultimate pragmatist, who has kept my thoughts grounded for more than thirty-five years, and Walter Jr., my patient mentor, who loved to hear me say, "Guess what?" because what came after that was always a zinger. Thanks for the many relationships I had during my Layline days, the teammates who helped shape my reality: Josh, Lori, Trish, Henry, Dewey, and Hahn. Also, thanks to the industry partners and competitors who drove me every day to be the industry leader, guys like Paul McKee and Keith Musto, Alistair Murray, Bob Bitchin, and the list goes on. Ron Sheeler, who said, "There is always room for another good one." Thanks to my crazy entrepreneurial ancestors who came over on the Mayflower as what the Puritans called Strangers, and my Honey Badger Tribe that led to the classes and continuing ed I have followed to become who I am today.

TABLE OF CONTENTS

PART III: ATTAINING AND MAINTAINING *YES*

ACKNOWLEDGMENTS

I WOULD ALSO like to acknowledge the many who have assisted and supported my efforts throughout the many years of my career. Those include the following:

Life:

Walter L. Brown Jr., Tom Gower, Carl Hudson, Ron Scheeler, Tee-Wee Blount, Dr. Randy White, Dr. Junius H. Terrell, Earl Johnson Jr. Olaf and Peter Harken, Paul McKee, Alistair Murray, and Bob Bitchin.

As a direct influence on this book:

Greg Walker, Don Tinney, Gino Wickman, Dan Sullivan, Patrick Lencioni, Dr. Dino Signore, Dr. John Grinnell, S. Covey, Maria Kingery, Bulldog (Jonathan Smith), Wildstyle (Jill Young), Clearman (Greg Cleary), MOD (Mark O'Donnell), Shrek (Chris White), Tom Bauer, Clay Gilbert, Marion Brown, Jane Brown, Rock (Duane Marshall), Alex Freytag, and Hurricane (Ken Dewitt).

And to all the teams who have traveled with me on their journey to championship form.

ABOUT THE AUTHOR

"SEASONED MULTI-COMPANY entrepreneur" is one label people have applied to Walt over the years.

Many folks refer to Walt as an entrepreneur, but he insists this is much too generous: "I don't consider myself an entrepreneur. I consider myself someone who is good at seeing existing patterns and pulling them together in logical ways that people are willing to pay for."

One trait that sets Walt's career apart from others is extreme seasonality. When one is in a seasonal business, two good, bad, and ugly things come with it: 1) The bad and ugly of the seasonal business are extreme cash-flow issues, 2) The good is the off-season, when you have time to think, plan, consider a serious change in approach, and then test the execution next season. Most companies do not have this luxury to think, plan, execute, observe, adjust, plan, etc. They also don't have to deal with the hurricane season or manage cash in a year when the spigot turns on in March and turns off in September. Walt was cursed and blessed with seasonality, and it provided him a unique number of reps to hone his understanding of strategic thinking and patience. The built-in patience of those cycles shaped Walt's business philosophy and his approach to team coaching, which puts patience front and center. During the last decade, he has helped transform the culture of more than one hundred twenty-five businesses across the country as an Implementer of the Entrepreneurial Operating System®.

In his current business life, Walt gets to ride along with his clients as they think, plan, execute, observe, adjust, and reflect while mastering the skills necessary to permanently enjoy the fruits of a Patient Organization.

ENGAGEMENT, DISCOVERY, AND THE MILLENNIAL MYTH

Engagement

IT IS TOLD that distinguished seventeenth-century architect Sir Christopher Wren shared a story about employee engagement. Yes, there was interest in employee engagement in the year 1678.

Wren, who was highly regarded for many of London's finest church designs, was visiting the job site of his St. Paul's Cathedral project in London.

His visit took him to the stone mason's pit.

He came upon a mason and asked: "What are you doing?"

The worker answered: "I am cutting these stones to a certain size and shape."

Wren asked the same question of a second worker and the worker answered, "I am cutting stones for a certain wage."

Wren came to a third mason and asked the question again. This time, the worker got up from what he was doing, straightened himself and replied: "I am helping Sir Christopher Wren build St. Paul's Cathedral."

This story hits my heart every time I think about it, because it is exactly the world and situation I am trying to help my clients create. I want their folks to stand tall and say that they are helping build the best company they can—that they are not, as Patrick Lencioni states, anonymous or irrelevant.[1]

On the scale of engagement, who would you say was the most engaged mason?

In our world of ICI (instant competitor imitation),[2*] the one thing that cannot be instantly copied are engaged employees. You know who they are—they are your folks who believe in your vision, assume accountability, live in a productive reasoning mode, are not fearful and defensive, who stand up, hold their shoulders back, and say I am part of the team and we are doing this together.

I train owners and leaders in the use of tools that allow them to consistently hire and motivate employees who stand tall and think of their work as more than their job. They are teammates on a team driving to a common vision, a common goal.

---

1   Patrick M. Lencioni, *The Truth About Employee Engagement: A Fable About Addressing the Three Root Causes of Job Misery* (Hoboken: Jossey-Boss, 2015).

2   * ICI - Instant Competitor Imitation: I lived in this world. My company, Layline, was the industry thought leader and what came with this were imitators/copycats, and with the advent of the Internet, the speed that a competitor could adjust to a message or offering was basically overnight. The only thing that allowed a gap was incredibly engaged teammates who added that special something, caring, whatever it might be, that the customers could feel and appreciate. Employee engagement is still the only defensible position against ICI.

Discovery and the Millennial Myth

The problem with millennials is...

You can complete that sentence any way you wish. Like all stereotypes it will be false and the odds are favorable that I've heard whatever you come up with. I am lucky—in a typical year I get to spend eight hours a day across 135 days huddled with senior leadership teams of thirty different companies doing the gutsy work of improving their organizations. The biggest problems at organizations involve people and through the years, I've noticed complaints about people often include the millennial stereotype excuse.

This confused me. Every week I worked with millennials who were part of my senior teams, millennials who are not only smart, engaged, and hard working, but also poised to take over the world. Why the disconnect? The teams and organizations I worked with did not share a bias against millennials. What was it that we were doing together that was breaking this millennial stereotype?

I started pulling these millennials aside, having discussions with them, trading thoughts and emails, looking for the pattern, probing for what made them different—what was breaking the mold? We distilled my analysis and used it to discover the *seven fundamental principles* that distinguished companies that were happy with their millennials from those that were not. From these principles came the *Seven Questions* at the heart of this book.

As we refined the Seven Questions (7Qs) and shared them with everyone from programmers, receptionists, and salespeople to CEOs and business owners, we realized we had discovered not just questions, but jewels. Everyone we tested the 7Qs on felt that we were getting at all of the things that motivated and engaged them at work. It did not seem possible to hit all the areas that would satisfy, inspire, and empower team members with just seven fundamentals, but as we looked for an eighth question, people told me again and again that we had covered all the bases with the 7Qs.

With the 7Qs, we discovered something equally as exciting as the solution to the millennial bias. It turns out that every team member wanted the same thing as a millennial did. They want to *belong*, to *believe*, and to *be accountable*. They want to be able to embrace the ways they are *measured* and to feel that they were *heard*. They wanted their organizations to offer opportunities for *development* and *balance*.

It was that uncomplicated. Seven simple principles. When we presented these principles in the form of questions, we realized that when leaders could get all team members to say *yes* in these seven areas, most of the complaints will disappear. The dysfunction would fade, and the organization would enjoy the kind of advantage that'd leave competitors dazed.

Digging deeper, we discovered the common thread tying these 7Qs together was Patience. Seven "yeses" built perseverance, wisdom, and grit into organizations. It helped them to establish an authentic vision, and create the goals and strategies to realize it. It created an approach that is best described as *patient*. Answering *yes* to the 7Qs makes you a Patient Organization.

I continued testing this thesis. As a team coach, I have worked with industrial rigging and construction companies, IT companies, software companies, for-profit healthcare businesses, a nonprofit battling homelessness, a boutique real estate brokerage, a local SPCA branch, ORNL (the national research lab), a tea company, a hair salon franchise, and many more. The 7Qs worked for all of them—enormous, tiny, for-profit, nonprofit. If your organization has people, the Seven Questions apply, and this book is for you.

I began posting the 7Qs on walls. I help leadership teams implement the Entrepreneurial Operating System (EOS®). This is a form of an *organizational operating system* (OOS). If you aren't familiar with the term, an OOS allows an organization to codify how it operates. A concrete set of OOS tools help owners set priorities, review team members, track numbers, develop marketing strategies, and communicate. I've used EOS® to help transform the cultures and boost the bottom-lines of more than one hundred and twenty-five companies.

Having the perspective of growing and running four companies of my own, I was smitten by the EOS® model and its results, but could never fully explain why it worked so well. Over time, I made yet another discovery: OOSs work because they answer *yes* to all the 7Qs. The tools of an OOS must help an organization maintain *yes* on the 7Qs, and the best OOSs leave no gaps.

The beauty of the 7Qs is in their thoroughness and simplicity. Only seven questions, a few words each, and yet they can transform an entire organization. This is not to say that getting to *yes* is easy. On the contrary—it's difficult, takes time, and often causes pain. My goal in this book is to make getting to *yes* as smooth as possible, so you can begin enjoying the advantages of a Patient Organization.

In Part I, I begin with some of the theory that underlies organizational life, OOSs, and my views of patience, leadership, and dysfunction. This is the 20,000-foot view. It's the shortest section because this is not a purely theoretical book. Part I is intended to be extremely practical, with common-sense thoughts you can begin using tomorrow.

In Part II, we'll roll up our sleeves to see how and why the 7Qs work, identify the obstacles to avoid, and supply a diagnostic to see how close or far from *yes* your organization is on each question.

Part III will help you understand how to get to the first *yes*, what I call the Heavy Lift, and what to look for in an OOS to help you maintain *yes*.

Patience is much more than a virtue. Instilled in an organization through the 7Qs, it is a way to motivate team members who belong and believe, to make decisions that align with your core values and your Why, and to realize a vision that makes you a fierce competitor.

PART I

DEFINING THE PATIENT ORGANIZATION

CHAPTER 1

THE BACKSTORY TO THE PATIENT ORGANIZATION

MOST ORGANIZATIONS BEGIN with a dream. Someone is passionate about a product, service, or cause and at some point, realizes they can provide it better or faster or cheaper than the next guy. Founders take on the considerable risk of starting businesses because they know they are good at this thing, whatever it is, and they have a vision for an organization—a dream. Most worked for others before striking out on their own and were dissatisfied, if not disgusted, with the way those companies operated—the mismanagement, missed opportunities, mistreatment.

So many misses!

The more they think about it, the more they yearn for the chance to have a hit, to build an organization on their values, one that will maximize profit and its people's potential. Their organizations will be innovative, react nimbly to markets, and grow at a steady clip. They will surround themselves with talented, hard workers and create the place where they always wanted to work.

For a while, sometimes many years, the dream inches toward reality. Founders surround themselves with hard workers who believe in the same thing, communicate well, and work together on targets.

Profits start to flow and the business grows. "Business" actually feels like the wrong word for what they're creating. This thing that began as a dream is alive and growing. This thing has a soul.

The team expands. Founders are no longer pleased with everyone, but maybe this is inevitable, just as growth was bound to make communicating tougher. It's hard to say exactly where or why communication is failing these days, but too many fires need dousing now to worry about that.

Profits aren't quite where the owners hoped, so they introduce various business school measures (there's now an MBA, or several in the picture). Improvement comes in fits and starts, but they keep bumping into that invisible something that drains the momentum, and they can't seem to break through. Key projects stall and important tasks slip. Too many employees lack drive and initiative. The status quo is seeping in. Owners have never worked harder or had less to show for their effort. They have never needed a vacation more, or felt less able to take one. Their stomachs churn at the thought that the horrible old cliché has come true—they aren't running the business, it's running them.

What happened to the dream? It has become something awful—a company, or worse yet, a business. The once-living thing has morphed into a soulless machine. Like a machine, it is static and rigid. It can't grow, evolve, or adapt, and founders aren't sure where things went wrong.

This is when I meet most of the people I work with—some desperate, others only dissatisfied, but all are aware of a significant gap between their original vision and the dysfunction they now see on a daily basis. The root of the problem—and the argument at the heart of this book—is that they are not running Patient Organizations. In this section, I will explain exactly what I mean by a Patient

Organization and introduce the Seven Questions that can transform even the most dysfunctional business into a Patient Organization.

In case the notion of Seven Questions implies otherwise, I want to point out right away that this is not an easy process. Just like Patrick Lencioni, author of *Five Dysfunctions of a Team,* says about core values, an organization considering the journey to become a Patient Organization must first come to grips with the fact that when properly done, it will inflict pain.[3] The Seven Questions will hold leaders to a higher standard and will make some of your teammates feel like outcasts. Getting back to your dream will not necessarily be a walk in the park. Some pain is unavoidable.

Patience, as I'll explore shortly, has nothing to do with dragging feet, suffering fools, or reacting sluggishly. A Patient Organization takes the time to focus, to rise above the system, to make methodical improvements, and to prioritize problems and opportunities. Patience leads to consistency and stamina, and it attracts employees who love their work. When team members and the business as a whole enjoy *yes* on the vital Seven Questions, they create a Patient Organization that runs smoothly and gains a massive edge over the competition.

Patience Is Industry Agnostic

My concept of a Patient Organization and the Seven Questions is the distillation of thirty years of experience—twenty growing my own four businesses, and another decade helping to transform the cultures of hundreds of companies as a team coach. This book is a

---

3   Patrick M. Lencioni, "Make Your Values Mean Something," Harvard Business Review, July 2002, https://hbr.org/2002/07/make-your-values-mean-something

one-size-fits-all solution. Issues and goals vary widely from owner to owner and business to business, but when someone asks what sorts of organizations the Seven Questions can help, I pretend to think deeply, then smile and say unironically, "the kind with people." Normally, this is followed by hearty laughter from both of us.

If that's the kind of organization you're running—the kind with people—this book is for you. In one recent week, I spent Monday with the leaders of the Wake County SPCA, which has seventy-eight people on payroll and hundreds of volunteers; Tuesday at an industrial rigging company that employs 1,180 people; Wednesday with an eighteen-person commercial real estate firm; Thursday with the team overseeing 781 people at the Oak Ridge Laboratory in Tennessee; and Friday with a team that runs five swim schools, with forty-eight people. All are benefitting enormously from embracing the Seven Questions as I help them become Patient Organizations.

As I often tell leaders, the language of a Patient Organization is industry agnostic. Small or enormous, for-profit or nonprofit, heavy manufacturing, software, or customer service—if the operation has people, running it well requires patience. Throughout the book, I will give concrete examples to show in practical terms how *aligning to yes* on the 7Qs can help all owners and leaders create Patient Organizations that align with their vision.

Every problem in an organization is, at root, a people problem. Corporations exist on paper, but they aren't real entities without the people who comprise them. As my father, a dedicated retailer running fourteen stores with twenty-one hundred employees used to say, "It would be easy if it weren't for the people."

As someone who coaches senior leadership teams as part of my EOS® Implementation Practice, no one knows this better than I do. I typically work with thirty or so teams at a time, meeting with each for five full days a year. This means that more than one-third of my days, around 135 per year, are spent in rooms with senior leadership. Most of the issues and problems we uncover during sessions ultimately have to do with people.

The frustration with people is understandable. According to a recent Gallup survey, around 70 percent of US workers are not actively engaged at work. Business owners often cite Gallup's famous engagement stats—some have them memorized—and all can supply anecdotal evidence of problems with team members and a work ethic that seems to have slipped.

This might be a good time to go to the stats. Every three years, Gallup does a US employee engagement survey, and the numbers look like this: 32 / 50 / 18 (see Figure 1).[4]

Nearly one-third of folks, 32 percent, are engaged to actively engaged. This is where the magic happens, where the new ideas are formed, where the profitable and creative relationships are established.

Half of the folks are just "neutrally engaged." There are a couple of awareness points I like to make with my clients around this 50 percent. One is that we have to have these folks. They are the coal cars in the coal train, happily carrying heavy loads, staying in line. They don't drag their brakes, but they don't add a lot of energy like the engaged "engines" do, either. We have them and need them, and we must embrace that they are just fine as neutrally engaged, and work to keep them happy.

The last group makes up 18 percent of workers and they are disengaged to actively disengaged. I ask when coaching if anyone knows who I am talking about, can they picture one of these faces,

---

4   Amy Adkins, "Employee Engagement in U.S. Stagnant in 2015," Employee Engagement, Gallup, January 13, 2016, http://news.gallup.com/poll/188144/employee-engagement-stagnant-2015.aspx

and almost 100 percent of the time, folks give a resounding yes. I also ask how many engaged team members does it take to offset a disengaged team member. Gallup says the ratio is 1:1, my clients say 3:1. One client, Michael, put it this way: "Let's have a race. I am going to run around messing up the house, and you go around, cleaning the house. Who is going to win?" Always gets a chuckle.

Why is someone disengaged? *Because they care.* (See They Care graphic.) Team members become disengaged because they care deeply about something that *you* are not providing. The answer is in the Seven Questions.

And yet when we pull the two ends together at the top of the accompanying circle graph, we see that the distance between engagement and disengagement is very small, and it is easier to lose someone to disengagement than it is to move a coal car to active engagement. Why? Because the people at the top care.

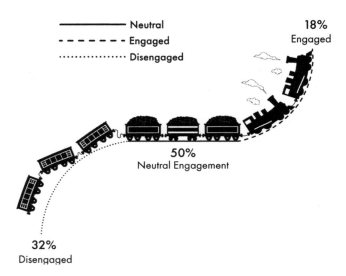

Figure 1. Statistics taken from Gallup employee engagement survey: 32 / 50 / 18 and combined with my perspective to illustrate this concept

"They Care" Graph

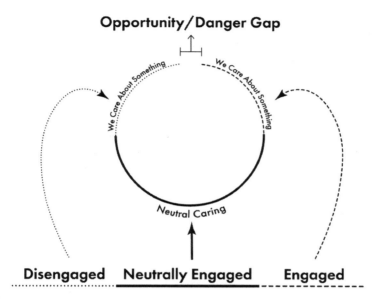

Opportunity/Danger Gap

We Care About Something

We Care About Something

Neutral Caring

Disengaged   Neutrally Engaged   Engaged

Don't waste your best efforts trying to move neutrally engaged folks to engagement. Work hard to keep the engaged folks engaged and to make the disengaged, engaged—or to get them to self-select out of your organization.

Final note: "You know, some people just be crazy." This pearl came from an Atlanta Uber driver who was quizzing me about what I do and the wisdom behind it—and he's right. There are some people you just cannot work with, and the Seven Questions will not fix them.

Millennials, who in 2017 ranged from college age to their mid-thirties, get a particularly bad rap. I won't repeat the stereotypes most readers have probably encountered when it comes to this generation. I don't for one second agree with the negative traits I've heard endlessly ascribed to them, but I understand business owners' concerns. In 2016, millennials accounted for 38 percent of the US workforce, and some estimate they could be 75 percent of US of the workforce by 2025.[5] The future health of our economy depends on harnessing the energy of these workers, so if they were particularly tough to motivate, owners would be right to worry.

At a quick glance, the Gallup stats might seem to back the stereotypes. Only 29 percent of millennials were engaged at work in 2016, according to Gallup's study, "How Millennials Want to Work and Live," and a record 60 percent of them are open to new job opportunities—a higher percentage than in any previous generations.[6] But when you look at the macro stats about engagement, you see the numbers are basically the same: 29 / 50 / 21. Damn, millennials are humans, too.

I would suggest, however, that while owners' complaints are understandable, the real causes of their frustrations are misunderstood. That gap between perception and reality actually became the foundation for this book and the start of a ten-year journey for me, doing soft-skills research, observing patterns, and building on decades of my own experience in business.

The spark that led to *The Patient Organization* was simply this: in my work with a wide range of organizations, the millennials I met were capable, talented team-players eager to take on leadership roles. I could not reconcile my experience of team members like Kerrie, a

---

5   Brandon Rigoni and Bailey Nelson, "Few Millennials Are Engaged at Work," Business Journal, Gallup, August 30, 2016, http://news.gallup.com/businessjournal/195209/few-millennials-engaged-work.aspx

6   "How Millennials Want to Work and Live," Gallup, 2016, https://enviable-workplace.com/wp-content/uploads/Gallup-How-Millennials-Want-To-Work.pdf

twenty-eight-year-old company president (not an owner or relative of one) doing an exemplary job of integrating an $8 million-per-year business with sixty-seven employees.

What inspired Kerrie and the other hardworking millennials I met and what made them actively engaged? I discovered that millennials, in fact, desire the same things we all do. The ones I spoke to wanted to be held accountable, and a lack of clear accountability left them frustrated. They wanted to feel like they were serving a larger purpose—don't we all?—but many of their leaders seemed unable to articulate their organization's *why*, or merely paid it lip service. The millennials I spoke to longed to feel confident in the ways they were measured and heard and developed. Leaders who provided that confidence through clear channels received a high level of engagement and performance in return. Those who did not blamed the confusion and frustration they sowed—often with the best of intentions—on the supposedly poor motivation of a generation.

I quickly came to realize that what I was learning about millennials applied to all team members, whether eighteen years old or eighty. They answered my questions about satisfaction and frustrations at work in many ways, some at length and some briefly, some with great precision, and others with vague unease. Some couldn't wait to go to work in the morning, and some expressed dissatisfaction, but the same patterns kept emerging.

After years of these discussions, I noticed that the important issues mirrored the same ones I'd encountered running my own four companies. I'd addressed them in various ways as a business owner, but had never spelled them out, as I was starting to do in my work with leadership teams. As a coach, I eventually was able to distill those years of feedback into the seven fundamentals at the heart of this book—the Seven Questions.

I will spend Part II exploring the Seven Questions in depth and devote Part III to strategies for *attaining and maintaining yes* on them. Each question has two parts. The first is for the organization and lays the groundwork for the second part, which team members ask themselves as they work to understand and embrace what yes means. Here are the Seven Questions, in brief:

THE SEVEN QUESTIONS (7Qs)

THE INDIVIDUAL MUST SAY YES, ABSOLUTELY, PART II	THE ORGANIZATION MUST SAY YES, ABSOLUTELY, PART III
1. Do I belong?	
I fit our organization's core values and have the skillsets needed for my job. I Belong.	We have clearly defined our core values and skills necessary for every position.
2. Do I believe?	
I am motivated by our why and the strategic direction leadership is taking. I Believe.	We know our *Why* and *Focus*, and have clearly laid out strategies that are consistently communicated.
3. Am I accountable?	
I understand the purpose of my job, and what I should be thinking and doing. I am Accountable.	Our accountability and responsibility structure is clear.
4. Am I measured well?	
I understand and embrace how I am Measured.	We have metrics for our positions. Owners use them to form strategies for success.
5. Is my opinion is heard?	
I understand and embrace how I am Heard.	We have clear communication— meetings, mentoring, etc.—to build trust, spur debate, and solve problems.
6. Am I developing?	
I understand and embrace how I am Developed.	We have a system that helps team members take charge of their development.
7. Do I have balance?	
I understand and embrace how Balance is maintained.	How we consider everyone's time and life capacity for work is clearly presented and systematic.

These seven principles, I discovered, were the things that made not just millennials, but all employees feel enabled and engaged. It made them love going to work. The questions were simple. Getting team members and the business to answer *yes* on all of them was not, but once I understood I had a key that could unlock success for any organization willing to use it, I knew I had to write this book.

Excited about the Seven Questions, I drilled down further and realized that *patience* is the foundation they rest on. Patience had been on my mind. In my conversations with millennials, I came to understand that if they differed at all from previous generations, it was perhaps because they had more clarity about what they wanted and a little more wisdom when it came to their futures. That wisdom gave them the patience to not simply accept the status quo or some prescribed route, or to take what someone handed them without the ability to change their circumstances. They were patient about shaping the right futures for themselves, and they thrived as members of Patient Organizations.

Pretty much every human I shared them with gave me an enthusiastic *yes* and agreed I was onto something—they did not see any holes or gaps. I was a good team coach before I had the Seven Questions, but using them with teams upped my game. They were direct and clear and made sense to everyone, from longtime business owners to new team members fresh out of school.

Attaining and Maintaining *Yes*

The Seven Questions felt almost magical to me for another reason, too. They explained how and why the things I did as team coach—and that I had done running my own businesses—worked. Let me back up here for a moment and explain briefly how I came to work as a coach for the clients I call PBOLTs—Private Business Owners with Leadership Teams (pronounced P-Bolts). In school, I studied business, accounting, and statistics. (Ironically, I am a guy that's dyslexic.) Straight out of school, I worked for a "Big 8" CPA firm for four audit seasons.

In 1986, I took the IQ exam and scored low enough that I was allowed to start my own company—that's a joke my wife, Anne, hates. I actually went into the mail order catalog business, selling stuff to households that included someone who raced sailboats. Readers of a certain age will remember that at the time, the Lands' End clothes catalog appeared poised to take over the world. My catalog ideas grew into the company Layline (a sailing term), which became a dotcom, and expanded into equestrian-related goods—on the premise that where there's smoke there's fire, and where there's a sailboat there's probably a horse.

Through the Layline catalog, I became good at finding European brands that wanted a foothold in the US. I would set up the company here and create distribution for them and then, basically, sell the business back to the brand. After years of doing that successfully, we captured the attention of a family office that bought Layline in 2006.

I was on the board of Sail America, our trade association at the time, and before I sold my company, I attended a board meeting where George, the guy who ran *SAIL* magazine, told us about the coach who helped with his strategic thinking and the peer board he relied on for consulting, a company called The Alternative Board (TAB). I loved the idea and was grilling him about it when lightbulbs went off around the table. "You'd be great at that, Walt," was the consensus.

George told me all about TAB, and soon after, I bought the franchise for the Raleigh-Durham area. A month after selling my businesses, I had twenty-seven TAB clients. I had success getting business owners on board with the TAB approach, which involves aligning personal vision with business vision, as well as following a strategic thinking method called "critical success factor" that I'm a big fan of.

Nine months later, pleased clients were saying that they knew where they wanted to go with their lives and businesses. Could I come in to meet with their leadership teams to help them pivot and turn the ship to get there? My own companies had been patient, nimble, and strategic, so I didn't hesitate to say yes—of course I could help them in the execution.

I went to six appointments with teams, where I presented this business school approach to strategic planning and at first, everyone around the table thought it would be great. By the time I was halfway through the sessions, though, they were staring at the ceiling, tongues lolling, clearly thinking, *oh no, another strategic planning retreat that's going nowhere.* Their frustration was palpable.

I did not have a concrete, strategic way to help my clients turn the ship, it turned out. I had made those pivots in my businesses numerous times, but I couldn't coach someone else on how to do it. I called my clients and told them I did not yet have a way to help them execute their vision, but I knew one was out there and I was determined to find it.

I dug in and read all the business books making waves then—*Good to Great, Built to Last, How the Best Get Better, The Five Dysfunctions of a Team, The E-Myth, In Search of Excellence,* etc. My reactions ran rampant—*no, not quite, good idea, interesting approach, horrible strategy* (no particular order here, just sharing my reactions). I learned a lot, but even the authors with valuable ideas were writing what I call 20,000-foot books. They all had views from an altitude of 20,000 feet, which looked beautiful (you can't see the graffiti and potholes from up there, right?), but no one was explaining how to make their vision happen on the ground.

Miraculously, this angel, Don Tinney, and this system called EOS®—the Entrepreneurial Operating System—found me online, and once Don laid out the EOS® model and its tools to me, I thought without hesitation, here it is. There is no need to look any further. EOS® gets to the heart of the mechanics and did what I did best in my businesses but couldn't communicate to my TAB clients. I knew in my gut that EOS® provided business leaders with a key first step, an implementable Organizational Operating System (OOS). I brought the system back to the half-dozen clients I'd put on hold and then ran another twenty-seven through an EOS® implementation over the next eighteen months. The results were so good that I sold my TAB practice to my partner, Keith, and hung my shingle as a focused EOS® Implementer.

I will explore EOS®, a.k.a. *Traction,* and other organizational operating systems in more detail in Part III, but briefly, a good OOS provides an efficient way for businesses to clarify exactly who is responsible for what and to focus the company's vision (why it exists, what it does, where it's going). It is the opposite of the intangible business school strategizing that caused my TAB clients' eyes to glaze over during my first ill-fated attempts to help them execute their vision.

A Patient Organization has to have an OOS—whether it's developed organically, ad hoc (as mine were, when I ran Layline), or imported with clearly articulated tools like EOS®, 4DX, Rockefeller Habits, Scaling Up, Holacracy, and others. Without one, leaders find themselves running from fire to fire, and strategic thinking suffers.

Accountability, metrics, purpose—all the keys to running a successful organization—suffer because patience is in short supply.

In my view, an OOS's purpose is to build patience into the organization—the difference between responding and reacting. Both involve taking action as a result of new developments or information, but reacting is defensive, rushed, uncontrolled, survival oriented, and often emotional. Responding is logical, thoughtful, data based, and goal oriented. Patience responds, panic reacts.

PATIENCE RESPONDS, PANIC REACTS.

During the last decade, as I helped transform the cultures of businesses through my EOS® work, I kept trying to understand exactly why EOS® works so well. This question was a constant companion running alongside my quest to understand what millennials want at work. I realized the answer to both quests was the same in the end—the Seven Questions. The seven key things that inspire millennials—and all workers—are also the hidden principles on which EOS® and a few other OOSs rest.

The tools of a good OOS must help a business *maintain yes* on the Seven Questions. If the system doesn't address and maintain all of the 7Qs, then the gaps eventually spell trouble for any business relying on it. I realize that the relationship between the two can sound a little circular, but I hope that it appears more and more symbiotic in Part II, as I explore the Seven Questions in depth, and in Part III, as I offer practical direction regarding what to look for in an OOS to help you *get to and maintain yes.*

CHAPTER 2

WHY PATIENCE IS THE KEY

I'VE INTRODUCED THE idea of a Patient Organization as a model for businesses, but what exactly do I mean by *patience*? I want to discuss my take on patience, since it is sometimes misunderstood. Dictionary definitions reference an ability to endure difficulties and to remain calm when faced with problems. The *Collins English Dictionary* offers "tolerant and even-tempered perseverance" as its first definition. Other words we associate with patience include moxie, grit, guts, sturdiness, calmness, wisdom, focus, awareness, confidence, and thought.

Explaining what I don't mean by patience is perhaps the best starting point.

Patience does not mean slowness. It often requires slowing down in order to focus, reflect, and prioritize, but the Patient Organization has a methodology that actually allows for smarter responses faster. Patience has nothing to do with foot-dragging, procrastination, or putting off important decisions. Patience means having a system and a set of decision matrices in place to make it easier to strike when the time is right, and at lightning speed, if necessary.

Patience does not mean putting up with jerks. No business owner starts out dreaming of surrounding himself with jerks, but jerks have a way of creeping into organizations over time. Jerks force leaders to spend hours keeping people happy. They rob organizations of time, energy, and patience. Ultimately, they manifest as what I refer to as "organizational terrorists," holding teammates hostage and destroying the culture owners once dreamed of. Jerks do not share the business's core values—and they must go. Tolerating jerks is charity and insanity, not patience.

Patience does not mean avoidance. Patience does not look for ways to go around things, it goes through them. Again, having a patient system in place allows leaders to make the tough calls rather than avoiding them, to trek down a difficult path rather than take a shortcut to avoid pain.

Patience is not passivity. Patience is extremely active. It is about doing, but the doing is always accompanied by thinking. Often it is downright aggressive as it confronts a problem or seizes an opportunity. Indecision is at the opposite end of the spectrum from patience. Inaction within a system is not patience. Patience comes from rising above the system to actively improve it.

What Is Patience in Business?

Steve Jobs might be the poster boy of patience. He was one of the most patient leaders I can think of—and one of the most active. He was thoughtful, figured out what he wanted and how to get there, and then attacked it with grit. Everyone knows his visionary role in bringing the personal computer to the mass market, but they forget that he also travelled through India, studying Zen Buddhism in search of enlightenment just before co-founding Apple. They remember his revival of the company in the 1990s and the cultural revolution he wrought, but forget that he spent a decade at the mostly unprofitable NeXT, Inc., trying and failing and trying again as he developed the vision that would ultimately lead to the iPod, iPhone, and a remarkable host of innovations.

Was Jobs aggressive? This is the guy who attacked Dell for making "un-innovative beige boxes" and proved a fierce competitor, but his decisions were made with calculation and deep reflection. He didn't just take the time to arrive at a vision of what people wanted; he had the patience to set up the system that could deliver it. For Jobs, that meant beginning with the customer experience— "what incredible benefits can we give to the customer?" —and working backward to the technology. A less-patient leader might have taken an easier, speedier approach by starting with the available technology and then thinking about the marketing and user experience.

Jobs is an abstract figure, though, and a myth to most of us. Think about a couple of favorite leaders who were in your life at some point. Consider their history and choices, how they interacted with others. Peel away the layers and you will see patience underneath. Your favorite coach, teacher, boss—odds are they were deeply patient. They probably surrounded themselves with others who were patient, too, people with the willingness and capacity to endure difficult and disagreeable circumstances.

Like Jobs, the patient leaders you're thinking of were likely quite active, but they saw the big picture and were methodical about achieving goals. Teaching children a new concept, building a winning sports team, or hitting a milestone in your market all require patience and an evolved system. Patient leaders, as I have noted, do not simply reside within a system, they step back from it and at some remove, they prioritize issues, problems, and opportunities. The

Seven Questions force team members to step out of the system and patiently assess everyone's role, including their own, as well as the organization's overall purpose.

Patience means clearly defining every job in a business—exactly what responsibilities attach to it, how is performance measured? This takes serious time and effort. Getting the team members who fill those jobs to answer *yes* to the first of the Seven Questions—*Do I belong?*—can also be difficult. Do they have the necessary skills? If not, where exactly are they lacking and can they develop them? This also asks, do they belong in terms of the organization's core values—not just its stated *why* but the means it has chosen to pursue that purpose?

The organization that has taken the time to attain *yes* on this question now has a trusted team member it can lead, rather than a supervised employee it merely manages. Leaders can be patient with the employee because goals, accountabilities, and metrics are clear, and effective communication has been built into the system. The employee who has embraced *yes* feels greater security and trust in the organization and, clear on exactly what she needs to be doing and thinking, can pursue goals with patience. Attaining and maintaining *yes* regarding the Seven Questions requires patience, but when everyone on the team is answering them in the affirmative, patience is part of the organization's DNA.

Not everyone will arrive at or be able to maintain *yes*. Eliminating those who are a poor fit, either because they're jerks and don't share core values or because they simply don't have the right skills or aptitude, can be tough. Square pegs have a way of becoming entrenched in round holes and throwing up all manners of smokescreens to hide shortcomings. But eliminating the jerks builds a reserve of institutional patience. Jerks breed impatience and slow the tempo for everyone. Unloading them creates a steady beat for the entire team.

Patience has a beat, a solid rhythm. Leaders start to hear it and feel it in their bones as they build it into an organization's core. *Tuesday is the day we talk about big issues. We might not mention them much during the rest of the week, but Tuesday's meeting is reserved for the big stuff. Monday mornings we review sales numbers. Once each quarter we spend a full day digging into our strategic plan.*

The ideal meeting structure varies from company to company, and I'll explore meetings in more depth later, but they are a great example of both the rhythm that patience establishes and the bird's-eye view it demands. Businesses need what Michael Gerber, author of *The E-Myth,* calls *In* meetings and *On* meetings. An *In* meeting covers "the old company" —daily operations, last week's numbers, this week's challenges—all the stuff that involves leaders working in the business. An *On* meeting covers "the new company" —improvements to process and people, adjustments that take us to the future. These allow leaders to work on the company, not just in it.[7]

A Patient Organization needs a regular rhythm of both *In* and *On* meetings, and it challenges these meeting and their rhythms by rising above the system. Why is the meeting called that? Should it be renamed to improve focus? Who is in it? Why? What's the goal? Patience prevents meetings from proliferating and drifting, and it can be the difference between having team members leave the room feeling frustrated and numb, or having them leave feeling that they have clarity and have had their voices heard.

The degree of patience in an organization shows not just in the meeting schedule, but in the way it conducts them, too. The

---

7   Michael E. Gerber, *The E-Myth: Why Most Businesses Don't Work and What to Do About It,* 2nd ed. (Pensacola: Ballinger Publishing, 2004).

impatient meeting is top-down and overdetermined. Attendees aren't always sure what type of meeting they're in or how it maps with the organization's *why*. For these and other reasons, including everything from the wording of the agenda to the tone and body language of leaders, attendees might be reluctant to speak up, take a chance, or make a mistake. The patient meeting gives all team members a chance to lead with their ideas. It makes room for dissonance, dissent, or mistakes. Consider a gaggle of geese deciding where to land. There's a whole lot of honking and clatter before a decision is made and then they move there together as a group.

For the geese to land and for team members to feel comfortable, there must be a high degree of trust. Earlier I noted that defining jobs clearly, including accountabilities and metrics, and getting teammates to understand and embrace *yes* on the first of the Seven Questions—*Do I belong?*—builds trust. In fact, all of the 7Qs do, which is why the Patient Organization reaps the benefits of deeply felt trust. The employee who knows exactly what he's responsible for, how he's measured, and how he's heard is not afraid to speak up, whatever the idea. He is also not afraid to say, *I don't know, I need help,* or *I screwed up*. He's not afraid to say *that's actually not a part of my job, it's yours*.

EATT—EVOLVE, ADAPT, TRUST, TRY.

Later, I'll explore organizational trust in more depth and the model I call EATT—evolve, adapt, trust, try. Team members must have a basic level of trust in order to try—to not just show up and check boxes, but to actually apply their creativity and full abilities to achieving goals. That sort of trying throughout an organization becomes a powerful force. It is part of why some organizations are so adept at evolving and adapting, while others ply the same ideas and methods right into extinction.

A thriving business needs a constant stream of good ideas and useful information to evolve, and patience is a funnel for both. It not only provides leaders with snapshots of particular moments in time, but its openness also attracts and gathers data that allows for better decisions. Patient leaders are constantly collecting info, and they have the systems in place to respond to it nimbly when the time is right. Think of the patient leader as having a total awareness of the game. He or she is always taking aim, always on point, and continually assessing, *do I take the shot, do I take the shot?*

A military concept known as the OODA loop is helpful here. The letters stand for *observe, orient, decide, act.* The construct was developed by military strategist Colonel John Boyd for combat, but is often referenced in business these days. People sometimes misunderstand the cycle, however, by focusing on rapid reaction. In Boyd's view, the second "O," *orient*, was the most important part of the cycle.[8] A team leader or member must have the patience to orient himself and the organization, to process what is observed, filter it through experience, and test it against objectives before deciding and acting.

Those who misinterpret OODA as being primarily about speed get trapped in an impatient cycle we might christen OR—*observe, react*—which proves every bit as leaden as it sounds. Making bad decisions quickly weighs an organization down. Going through every part of the cycle and taking the time to *orient* ultimately provides agility and leads to decisions that are smart and as fast as they need to be. It's understandable that the vital second *O* often gets short shrift. As Henry Ford said, "Thinking is the hardest work there is, which is the probable reason why so few people engage in it."

---

8   Frans P.B. Osinga, *Science, Strategy and War: The Strategic Theory of John Boyd* (Abington: Routledge, 2006).

An English friend of mine, Paul McKee, refers to the impatient, those engaged in OR, as "busy fools," and Paul does not suffer fools well. In a conversation one day, he described a particular company as "just a bunch of busy fools." I laughed and asked what he meant. "You know," he said in disgust, "busy, busy, busy. Those people who are always rushing around, never taking time to think." For some in business, everything is urgent and must be done yesterday. People in this mindset mean well and are working hard—often too hard and on the wrong things. They confuse urgency with importance. Patience is the filter that allows us to isolate the truly important and go after it in a considered, methodical way.

Patience is a big idea with many facets. I hope that in this section I've clarified what I mean by patience. Here are a few more reflections:

- Patience is something you have when you are working inside your unique ability.[9]

- Patience is a mental and physical manifestation of mastery, often called wisdom.

- Patience can be calm.

- Patience is proactive, a willingness to be present and in the moment.

- Patience focuses on the important—not everything should be urgent.

- Patience is creative, not reactive.

- Patience is the opposite of panic.

- Patience is the manifestation of clarity.

---

9   Dan Sullivan, *How the Best Get Better* (Strategic Coach Inc., 2001).

- Patience comes when you know what you want and are focused on it.

- Patience can be aggressive in going after a problem or opportunity.

- Patience takes the time to do the hard work and hard thinking, to make the hard call.

- Patience approaches, fear avoids.

- Patience creates, fear reacts.

- Patience controls passions, providing the courage to slow down and think.

- Patience means being aligned, accountable, authentic, and aware.

I will return to that last point and what it means to be *aligned, accountable, authentic,* and *aware*—the 4 As—later in the book. I will also return to the following idea, which readers should hear in the high voice of that famous strategic coach from another galaxy, Yoda: With patience comes consistency; with consistency comes stamina; and with stamina comes great, repeatable results.

THE FAMOUS STRATEGIC COACH, YODA, FROM ANOTHER GALAXY SUGGESTS: WITH PATIENCE COMES CONSISTENCY. WITH CONSISTENCY COMES STAMINA; WITH STAMINA COMES GREAT, REPEATABLE RESULTS.

CHAPTER 3

AN ORGANIZATION IS
A SHARED BELIEF

I HAVE DEVOTED considerable space to the idea of patience because, well, I'm an actively patient guy, and also because I believe it is the key ingredient in turning a decent organization into a champion or saving one that's gone off the rails. I'd like to briefly explore the second half of this book's title too. Most of my readers are business leaders, so why not *The Patient Business*?

For starters, that would be too narrow. As I said early on, the Seven Questions can transform any entity that involves people—a business, of course, but also a nonprofit, a trade association, or a university. I work mostly with businesses, but I also coach nonprofits, laboratories, and other organizations, and all benefit tremendously from the 7Qs.

A more important reason for the word *organization* is that it emphasizes structure, cohesion, and interaction—not products or services. It emphasizes people, and the Seven Questions are about how people come together around core values to fulfill a common purpose. Without their people, organizations are fictitious and exist only on paper.

To state the obvious, people can do incredible things when they unite and organize around a shared belief. In his popular and controversial book, *Homo Deus*, Yuval Noah Harari argues that much of mankind's dominance on earth comes from an ability to organize around shared meaning. Consider the great organizing principles of human societies, things like money, borders, religion, and national identity. They are useful only because groups of humans have *decided* they have meaning, Harari writes. Once people buy in and organize around such shared beliefs, great things become possible—complex economies, empires, technology, revolutions.[10]

An organization is essentially a fiction, only given meaning and power by those who believe in it.

Language itself marks a turning point in this phenomenon of *intersubjectivity*, a fancy word for social or shared meanings, closely related to the idea of consensus. You will hear me repeat that we all must agree on what words mean for language to work, and once we do, man makes unparalleled progress through the ability to record and transfer knowledge, to communicate complicated thoughts and concepts.

AN ORGANIZATION IS ESSENTIALLY A FICTION, ONLY GIVEN MEANING AND POWER BY THOSE WHO BELIEVE IN IT.

Forgive the philosophical tangent, but it gets to the root of what organizations are—and why they fail. If an organization, as a group of people united around shared beliefs for a common purpose, can achieve great things, it can also implode if its beliefs grow hazy or its purpose becomes unclear. When an organization does not convey a

---

10   Yuval Noah Harari, *Homo Deus: A Brief History of Tomorrow* (New York: Harper Collins, 2017).

clear purpose and core values, or harbors people who don't believe in them, dysfunction quickly follows.

On a more day-to-day basis, it is well documented that when humans form into groups, they can solve very complex problems as long as they can agree on how they name the problem and the words and language around the problem. Words and precise usage of language are the keys to solving complex problems and staying focused. If someone on your team will not agree to the jargon and terminology of the organization, then that person does not believe and will destroy efforts to attack issues, ultimately holding the organization back.

The weak links on a team not only turn in subpar performances, but they also infect their teammates and the entire organization. The intersubjectivity that has allowed humans to rule the earth allows for a crippling transfer of negative energy, too. Maybe this sounds a little New Agey, but we've all experienced the way that one person's bad attitude or lack of conviction can affect even the most enthusiastic team players. If enough people stopped believing in money, it would soon become simply paper and the economy would crumble. When people don't believe in the same borders—think Cyprus, Northern Ireland, the Middle East—tensions rise and hostility, even war, can break out.

Like money and political systems, an organization is a fiction, given meaning and power by those who believe in it. If some members don't believe, the organization suffers. If enough stop believing, it disappears.

Often, the team members who don't buy in are hard workers with good intentions, or at least, they started out that way. It's hard for them to believe that if leaders don't clearly communicate the beliefs at the heart of the organization's existence. Leaders might fall down here because they themselves are hazy on the true purpose and core values, apart from some dusty, awkwardly worded mission statement, or they might know the *why* but not spell it out in meaningful ways. Language is our greatest example of intersubjectivity, the force behind tremendous achievements and the font of our greatest failures.

It's no accident that the first two of the Seven Questions are *Do I belong?* and *Do I believe?* These are existential questions in the truest sense. For the organization, they force the clear definition of every role, "seat," or job, as well as its core values and its *why.* The words must be agreed on, written out, and communicated clearly to the entire team. For team members, the first question—*Do I belong*— asks not only if they have the necessary skills for a particular job, but more fundamentally, if they also share the organization's core work values. The second question—*Do I believe?*—spells out the organization's purpose and asks team members if they are motivated by it and the strategies used to achieve it.

Neglecting to ask these two fundamental questions risks dysfunction and infecting the team with malignant members who don't belong or don't believe in the mission. That's not all—the danger runs even deeper. Organizations, as I've argued, are fictitious. They exist only because of their members' belief in a shared purpose and values. Without that belief, they run the risk of extinction. They can grow meaningless over time, just as other shared human constructs— Zimbabwe's currency, Soviet borders, the Cornish language—lost their relevance when people ceased to believe in and belong to them.

The rest of the Seven Questions largely focus on communication and support the first two. Language is our prime example of and chief vehicle for shared meaning, so communicating effectively is a major part of human achievement. It's no accident that the presidents who ushered in the most sweeping changes in American society—leaders such as FDR and Ronald Reagan—were also among the best communicators.

Questions three and four are: *Do I know what I am accountable for, my purpose?* and *Do I agree with how I am measured?* It's tough to believe deeply in a purpose and a set of core values if you're not sure exactly how you are supposed to be contributing or don't have a fair mechanism for getting feedback on those contributions. Has the organization communicated both of these clearly and listened to team members' reactions? How closely are leaders listening to team members overall? The fifth question explores this necessary condition for getting teammates on board: *Am I heard?* The final two questions—*Am I developing?* and *Do I have balance?*—focus on key benefits and effects of the organization on team members' lives, not only highlighting important reasons for belief, but also how well the organization is expressing them.

As Harari demonstrates in *Homo Deus,* humans who come together around a shared belief are capable of astonishing accomplishments. America did not exist until a group of people decided they *believed in* and *belonged to* this ambitious undertaking called the United States. Part of their motivation had to do with feeling that their voices weren't heard and that they weren't treated fairly, so they experimented with the best ways to build that participation into the system. In a real sense, they strived to create a Patient Organization, with clear rights and responsibilities, where people could believe and belong and be heard.

Two centuries later, this new organization became the most prosperous nation on earth. The story of the Roman Empire is similar, but becomes a cautionary tale of what can happen when the *why* fades—core values are corrupted, and too many team members no longer believe.

The Seven Questions offer the clearest way to get and maintain shared belief in an organization's values and mission. They are the best mechanism to leverage language—the most powerful human example of shared meaning—to achieve incredible results.

Leveraging the Power of a Patient Leadership Team

I can already hear some readers saying, "A business is not a democracy." True, but patient leadership operates on many of the same principles—first and foremost the idea that people must believe and feel that they belong and have their voices heard for the project to thrive. Both are also perpetual works in progress, growing and evolving over years. Maintaining a *yes* to the Seven Questions, building belief and belonging, and establishing clear metrics and communication channels takes significant time and work, and the effort must continue even after a solid system is in place.

Leaving behind the European model of monarchy, our Founding Fathers settled on a system that fell short of pure democracy but gave a voice to the average person. It established a strong central government but reserved significant powers for the states, allowing them independence on many fronts. That decentralization, turning over power and accountability, is similar to the approach organizations need to get to *yes* on the Seven Questions and build strong leadership teams.

Unfortunately, the ability to empower a leadership team reflects a skill, or gift that many private business owners don't have. Some acquire it over time, others never do. In my experience, the first group tends to be happier, have lower blood pressure, and less gray hair. As a coach, I call them PBOLTs—private business owners with leadership teams—and they account for most of my client base. I work with the second group—PBOs, or private business owners—too, when they are making an effort to become PBOLTs.

Most leaders running small businesses begin as PBOs and maintain that approach until they hit a certain age and/or size. Strategic coach Dan Sullivan argues that in our early years, we are Rugged Individuals, learning as we go and taking on everything ourselves. There's nothing we can't do, and we try to do it all. At some point, though, we get a little wiser and discover our *unique ability*, the thing we do best. If I spent all my time focused on my unique ability, I could accomplish great things, and if I could surround myself with people who also are focused on their unique abilities, which are not mine, I could bore a hole in the universe!

This is the point when many business owners engage and excel. They go from being PBOs, or private business owners, to PBOLTs, private business owners with leadership teams. A PBO will describe his or her organization as "open-door and flat." This is a nice way of saying, *I make every damn decision and carry the weight of the entire company on my breaking back.* There isn't much of a hierarchy or accountability structure. PBOs fight every fire from their fireboats, racing across the harbor to save the day, completely unaware of the huge wake they leave behind. Things don't move up a chain very well; they simply roll straight across the floor to the owner's door, which is always open.

PBOs are usually knowledgeable, skilled, and ambitious. They aim for 100 percent, and often get it when they work on something, but they don't realize that a team of ten people, each taking the same number of shots as the owner and hitting 80 percent on the court, will kick the butt of one person hitting every shot.

PBOs become PBOLTs, or try to, when they hit this tipping point and realize they are holding the organization back. I say "try" because the transition is difficult and frequently fails. Many PBOs have the scar tissue to prove it, and after enough cuts they retreat from building true leadership teams.

Over decades of growing my own businesses and helping to transform others, I have had a front-row seat at dozens of these PBO to PBOLT transitions and have seen the same mistakes repeated over and over. Owners sincerely try to empower their people and install a new structure, but they are not systematic about determining who does and does not belong. They are not strategic enough or clear enough in communicating the big goals and how to get there. They do not spell out to team members exactly what positions they're *accountable* for, how they're being *measured*, and the ways they're being *heard*.

> A PBO WILL DESCRIBE HIS OR HER ORGANIZATION AS "OPEN-DOOR AND FLAT." THIS IS A NICE WAY OF SAYING, I MAKE EVERY DAMN DECISION AND CARRY THE WEIGHT OF THE ENTIRE COMPANY ON MY BREAKING BACK.

The problem is that owners are not answering the 7Qs or building patience into their leaders or their organizational structure. In fact, they are building a house of cards. It crumbles, and they get wounded. They might make another attempt by installing a COO or someone with a similar title meant to right the ship. This person often succeeds only in screwing up the organization's balance and inflicts even more suffering on owners. Finally, scraped-up and bloody, PBOs wind up going back to what they have always done—everything.

Owners need an Organizational Operating System to make this complex switch to becoming a Patient Organization, and the Seven Questions provide the roadmap. I felt thrilled to arrive at the 7Qs not only because they were the culmination of a journey that took years—really, a lifetime in business—but also because when I introduced them to PBOLTs, they immediately got it, agreed, and said that they did not see any gaps. Owners who do the hard work with both team members and their organization to understand and maintain an affirmative *yes* have built patience into their structure and are ready to cream the competition.

The process is painful at times and requires growing reserves of patience. The oft-used metaphor that a business is the owner's baby rings true, and owners must be ready to call on the kind of patience that a parent shows a child. It's not easy watching your child fall, but it's the only way he or she will learn to walk or ride a bike. All parents feel the urge to dote on and protect their children, but if we want them to be strong and independent, we learn to back off.

What if the team is not ready for that sort of independence, is not ready to answer the Seven Questions? Owners frequently ask this, and I answer that in my experience, the team is always ready. The direction rests with owners, and once they make the decision to run a Patient Organization, the team will follow. Not everyone, of course. The 7Qs will weed out those who don't belong, or as often happens, provide the mechanism that allows them to self-select out.

The good news is that most team members are ready to be led. They are ready for a change, ready to be part of a more cohesive team, and ready for clearer communication. Remember the much-maligned millennials who inspired this book by disproving negative stereotypes every time I worked with them. In my years of conversations and email exchanges with those fresh team members, I found that they were not only ready for the Seven Questions, but they were also hungry for the direction, accountability, metrics, and openness they provide.

The real question: is the owner ready to become a leader of a Patient Organization?

Management Is Not Leadership

The biggest complaint and the root of all other complaints is people—politics, infighting, poor communication, poor performance, lack of initiative, lack of control, no accountability, and a weak work ethic. My father's old saying, "It would be easy if it weren't for the people," is always true because organizations are their people. I have pointed out how the Seven Questions shore up organizations and build patience, but the 7Qs do something else too: they allow owners to lead, not just manage.

What's the difference? *Management is about doing.* It takes care of the day-to-day and the week-to-week: last month's sales numbers, training on new equipment, soothing an angry customer, reassigning Dave's duties while he recovers from surgery. It is today-focused and leans on the objective. *Leadership is about thinking and the big picture.* Where do we want to be in ninety days, one year, three years? What's our strategy moving forward, and how can it be improved? How has our mission, our *why,* changed and how should we communicate that to our team members, our clients, and other stakeholders? Leadership is subjective and future-focused as it creates the opening others will see and fill. Gino Wickman, creator of EOS®, was the first person to point this distinction out to me. He captures the full thought with an EOS® tool called LMA˜ (Leadership + Management = Accountability). I highly recommend Gino Wickman's and his sidekick Rene Boer's influential book on this topic, *How to Be a Great Boss.* It is one of those lessons that, once you hear it, drives you crazy when you hear others interchanging the words leadership and management. You know how I am about words.

A high percentage of small business owners spend so much time working *in* their business, to borrow Michael Gerber's frame once again, they have no time to work *on* it. A Patient Organization makes the time to work *on* the business too. It allows leaders to think and lead, and not merely to do—to manage. The organization that begins to use a solid operating system and to answer the Seven Questions is empowering a true leadership team.

For instance, the first question for team members—*Do I belong?*—can't be asked until the organization has clearly defined its core values and every job. The second question for team members—*Do I believe?*—is predicated on the organization's *why.* To answer the question, the organization must reflect deeply on and communicate its *why,* its focus, and a clearly laid-out strategy. Answering the questions elicits total alignment from team members, putting everyone on the same page as they work toward shared goals, but it also allows leaders to lead by forcing them to think about the organization's big picture and strategic direction. The Seven Questions require stepping back from the day-to-day to think about the future and the strategies that get us there, forcing leadership.

> **THE SEVEN QUESTIONS REQUIRE STEPPING BACK FROM THE DAY-TO-DAY TO THINK ABOUT THE FUTURE AND THE STRATEGIES THAT GET US THERE, FORCING LEADERSHIP.**

This process raises levels of productivity and investment for everyone around the owner, and it also gives everyone in the organization the opportunity to lead. Earlier, I used the example of a gaggle of geese honking away while they decide where to land as a metaphor for a good meeting. As geese make their famous V-shaped formation in midair, they also take turns moving to the front of the flock. Everyone gets a chance to lead, to think at some level. The same becomes true of a Patient Organization as it works through the Seven Questions. When people feel that they belong and they believe and they understand how their voices are heard, the culture blooms with confidence, ownership, and creativity. Team members stop shifting blame and start to take chances and express ideas. They feel a higher degree of trust, and they begin to lead, to think, not just to do.

Humans want to work in an atmosphere of trust. They want to feel that their work matters. They want to belong, to believe, to have their voices heard, to have clear accountabilities and be measured fairly. The Seven Questions transform organizations because these principles are built on the notion that an organization is its people. Since they are alive, the organization in a very real sense is alive too. It must adapt and evolve, and it must be treated like a living thing, not the soulless machine so many businesses become.

A business that is not growing and evolving is dying, or it's in hibernation. I talk to leaders about their organizations as living organisms when explaining the cycle that I mentioned earlier: EATT—evolve, adapt, trust, try. Businesses that don't evolve get left behind by their competitors and face possible extinction in a process very much like natural selection (in business, as in nature, only the ones most suited for their environment, the fittest, survive). To evolve, a business must adapt—tailor its efforts to a changing marketplace, new demands, developing technology, etc. Adaptations must be tried to figure out which ones work, and trying requires that individuals and teams trust that they won't be punished for taking risks and testing ideas.

I like the evolution metaphor because it highlights the danger of plodding along, managing without leading, and running an impatient organization—the path dinosaurs took, until it ended. Evolution also implies an ongoing process, not a simple project. Man evolved over the course of millions of years. Great organizations aren't born overnight, either. When I coach clients, I tell them that while they'll see some benefits quickly, the transformation into a Patient Organization takes, at a minimum, a couple of years, and more likely three.

The process begins with asking the Seven Questions. They are simple and user-friendly and make sense to both team members and leaders. They are also thorough. Asking them requires significant work on the part of the organization as well as its members. I will devote Part II entirely to asking the 7Qs, beginning with their antecedents in behavioral economics and neuroscience before exploring each question in depth. For each one, I'll explain the work that it does, list the "Patience Destroyers" that make *getting to and maintaining yes* difficult, and provide a reflection that helps leaders apply the theory behind the question to their organizations in concrete terms.

The dream of the entrepreneur might seem dead once control has slipped and the culture has drifted, but the Seven Questions can revive it by building a patient system. Imagine an organization where everyone is a patient thinker and doer, believing and belonging, and excited to come to work. Picture a place with a steady rhythm, a culture of trust and open, honest debate, with everyone aligned and accountable. An organization like that can achieve amazing results and effortlessly stomp its impatient competitors.

PART II

EXPLORING THE SEVEN QUESTIONS

CHAPTER 4

ANSWERS ARE EASY WHEN THE QUESTION IS CLEAR

AFTER I STARTED my first company, employees who had been around a while sometimes brought up "the speech" I gave when I hired them. At first, I wasn't sure what they meant—in most ways, they were more aware of my leadership style back then than I was— but when I thought about it, I realized that there was a consistent rap I delivered to potential hires during the interview process. One such interview with a former member (known as "Chief" of the Harvard sailing team) went something like this:

Chief, your qualifications look terrific. You did well at Harvard and you have great experience sailing. You seem like you would be a perfect fit, but before you say yes, I want you to think about some things. Consider what I'm about to say, sleep on it, and make sure you understand it. Every day when you walk through that door I want you to bring a positive, cheerful attitude. I do not want to be surrounded by a bunch of Debbie Downers. That does not mean ignoring problems or pretending. I expect you to be cognizant of each situation, too. You need to get serious when the situation demands it, but typically, we want to operate in a positive and cheerful manner. Also, we value listening here.

We strive to really understand each other, our customers, and our vendors and one way we do this is by trying to always ask three questions first, especially with customers. With the best of intentions, people often want to give customers input without having the full picture. We avoid this by attempting to ask three questions before we answer one. You'll learn more about this over time. Be sure to ask Henry and others for their take on it as you continue your interview rounds. We believe that the only dumb question is the one you don't ask. This ethos is important enough that we have an acronym for it around the office—PC3: be Positive, Cheerful, Cognizant, and ask three questions first. I also want you to Challenge your work. Try to understand why you're doing something and if it seems off, say, "Doing it this other way would make more sense." If you are using PC3 and challenging your work, you'll be a great team member. Everyone will love you and you'll excel here (Chief did excel).

I included this speech because so many of my readers will recognize that they have a similar interview rap, though like me at my first company, they might have spent little time reflecting on it. The roots of this speech and my acronym, PC3, actually go back to my college years. It was then that I decided that these were three qualities I valued.

P + CHEERFUL, COGNIZANT, CHALLENGE + 3 QUESTIONS = PC3

I wanted to be positive, cheerful, and cognizant, and even at that young age, I realized that I wanted to surround myself with people who were PC3 too.

After college, as I said, I worked for a Big 8 CPA firm for four audit seasons. The firm had many fine attributes, however, leadership did not put a premium on team members being positive, cheerful, and cognizant. Some of the impetus for starting my own company— that entrepreneurial dream I explored at the start of Part I—had to do with building an organization where I could surround myself with people who were PC3.

As the interview talk above demonstrates, I worked at finding PC3 team members, and I promoted that attitude within the organization. Unfortunately, this mostly meant hanging poster-board with "PC3" emblazoned on it around the office. One obstacle to fully realizing the dream for me, as for most entrepreneurs I meet, was a lack of awareness. I had core values—the heart of our first Question, *Do I Belong?*—but never recognized that this was what they were. I never named them "core values" and, so, never made them quite the priority I should have.

I talked some about the importance of language and naming things accurately in Part I, and I will return to that theme throughout the book. Failing to recognize and name PC3 as my core values meant that I did not integrate them into every layer of the organization. I mentioned them frequently, but without calling them core values and building them into a system, I couldn't really give them teeth. I did not yet know how to do that. I did not yet have the Seven Questions.

I had questions and was adamant my team members should have them too. It's interesting for me, looking back, to see my obsession with asking critical questions was already a part of the formula. I suppose I have always felt that, in a way, answers are the easy part. Well, not exactly easy—good answers require sweat—but with time, hard work, and a solid team, most of us can find good answers. The real challenge is asking the right questions.

My whole rap about being positive, cheerful, and cognizant; asking customers three questions first; realizing the only dumb question is the one you don't ask; and continually challenging your work all boils down to the first of the Seven Questions: *Do I Belong?*

For team members, asking, them that question would have meant testing how well they fit the core values and how well their skills fit their positions.

Getting to *yes* on the question *Do I belong?* would have given our core values teeth and integrated them into every facet of the organization. This, in turn, would have fostered patience by weeding out those who did not belong (the worst patience destroyers), clarifying accountabilities, and providing a touchstone against which strategy could be measured. *We're faced with a tough decision? Okay, well, let's think about how each possible choice maps with our core values.*

Like many entrepreneurs, I was in the neighborhood on this and many other fronts. Did I have core values? Absolutely. But I did not integrate them fully or have my ideal team because I was not asking the right questions.

Just Semantics? It's *All* Semantics

A lot of books about business, leadership, and management attempt to supply answers. Some offer good advice, but, frankly, you should be a little suspicious of anyone who doesn't know you, your field, or your organization trying to provide you with answers. Whatever your bailiwick—designing software, ending homelessness, producing widgets for helicopters, producing financial plans, setting up cranes— you know more about it than I ever will, and I would not presume to feed you answers.

This book is different because my sole goal is to help *you* ask the vital questions. You have the answers, just as I had core values without really knowing it. You too have core values and an organizational purpose. You have expertise, priorities, and goals. The answers are floating around the organization, and if your leadership team is remotely like the hundreds I have interacted with over the years, they're not asking the fundamental questions that create a Patient Organization.

A common response at this point is that what I'm arguing is "just semantics." I had core values at my first company, so what if I did not call them that? Calling someone an "undocumented worker" or an "illegal alien" in a newspaper article is just semantics, but that word choice frames the debate and conveys a world view.

Semantics is the branch of logic and linguistics that deals with meaning. This includes the relationship between words and what they stand for and, more broadly, between any sign and the things it signifies. The fact that people brake at "Stop" signs instead of accelerating through the intersection is "just semantics."

> CALLING SOMEONE AN "UNDOCUMENTED WORKER" OR AN "ILLEGAL ALIEN" IN A NEWSPAPER ARTICLE IS JUST SEMANTICS, BUT THAT WORD CHOICE FRAMES THE DEBATE AND CONVEYS A WORLD VIEW.

Does it matter whether team members call those who come to your organization *customers, clients, users, members,* or something else? Of course, in ways subtle and not so subtle, that label will shape every interaction they have. The difference between the motto Apple rolled out in 1997, *Think different,* and IBM's motto, *Think,* was a small, merely semantic difference, a single word that signified an innovative philosophy, billions in profit, and, ultimately, market dominance.

Not only does semantics matter, *it's all semantics.* Recall my argument in Part I that **an organization is essentially a fiction that is given meaning and power by those who believe in it**. If that's the case, what happens when things aren't named correctly or when team members use conflicting language to describe things? Consider the difference it would have made if I had impressed on every job candidate at my first company that PC3 represented our *core values*, and we hired and fired around them rather than just saying it was what I expected. When one team member sees something as a "motto," another as a "guideline," a third as a "slogan," and a fourth discounts it as mere cheerleading, that doesn't just mean poor cohesion within the organization. You have four people *believing* four different things. Since the organization quite literally is its members' beliefs, you have four different organizations.

The Seven Questions should guide you to embrace an OOS that forces you to investigate and articulate things you have taken for granted or neglected to reflect on, and they force you to use precise, accurate language to describe them. *These four things constitute our core values. We have painstakingly crafted them and reached agreement on the language and now, we can have team members ask, **Do I belong?** to this actual and singular organization, not fifty or five hundred different versions of it.*

When I work with senior leadership teams, I'll ask eight of those team members, *what is the purpose of the organization?* I typically get eight answers. When I ask about accountabilities, measurement, and how opinions are heard, I also get as many answers as there are respondents. Setting strategy, achieving goals, and building crack teams at one organization is difficult. It's impossible when you have eight disparate organizations, conflicting fictions, housed under one roof.

To solve a problem, as I said in Part I, people must first name it and agree on the language surrounding it. Doing this well is not easy, and it's not a merely *pro forma* step. Language reflects thought. Sloppy, impatient language reflects sloppy, impatient thought. The Seven Questions provide a path to patient, clear thought that produces accurate, specific language for everything from an organization's overall purpose to how the Tuesday meeting gets named.

System 1 Thinking, System 2 Thinking, and Getting SCARFed

My own fuzzy language around PC3—not naming it "core values"—created a gap I wasn't aware of, though I sensed its effects. Most organizations are full of such hidden gaps. Leadership teams think their meeting structure is just fine. They have a reporting hierarchy in place that they imagine takes care of accountability, and they would generally give themselves passing grades for how they measure, hear, and help develop team members.

And yet they hire me because there is a gap between the owner's dream and the actual daily dysfunction proliferating within the organization. That overall gap is composed of many smaller gaps that go unnoticed and unaddressed. The Seven Questions, coupled with an effective Organizational Operating System, offer a systematic way to find and address the gaps. As we explore the Seven Questions, I will include a reflection, "Diagnosing Patience," to help you reveal those gaps and measure how close you are to "yes" on each question.

After years spent discovering the Seven Questions, I knew I was onto something when I began presenting them to business owner friends and leadership teams at the organizations I coached. Immediately, I got enthusiastic nods and lightbulbs went off around the room. One day, I had lunch with a potential client and explained to him that a good Organizational Operating System works because it gets everyone to answer *yes* to these Seven Questions. The idea instantly grabbed him, and he insisted I email him the list. Leaders not only get the 7Qs, but they also agree that the list, because of the ways the questions overlap, leaves no gaps. They understand immediately that it will make their jobs and lives easier. These seven categories and an effective OOS cover everything you need to become a Patient Organization and leave your competition in the dust.

Why do the Seven Questions work so well? As I said in Part I, this is not one of those books with a 20,000-foot view, full of interesting theory and no way to implement it. *The Patient Organization* is meant to arm you with concrete questions and tools, but some readers aren't convinced until they see what's under the academic hood. For them, I will briefly touch on the philosophical and psychological underpinnings of the Seven Questions here.

The Seven Questions close gaps, force precise language, and build patience partly by shifting leaders and team members into what Daniel Kahneman, winner of the Nobel Prize in Economics, calls "System 2 thinking." Whereas *System 1 thinking* is fast, automatic, intuitive, emotional, and often irrational because it is often the easy, lazy path, *System 2 thinking* is patient, analytical, logical, rational, and difficult—the hard path.

Kahneman became the father of behavioral economics—quite a feat for a psychologist—partly as a result of his surprise at discovering how most economic models assumed that people were rational. Psychologists have long known that much of our thinking is instinctual, fast, irrational, and driven by bias, yet thinkers in economics and business often started with the idea of humans as driven mostly by rational, analytical thought, a view now widely discredited. Humans are typically lazy and fearful, they take the easy way, which is often irrational.

SYSTEM 1 THINKING	SYSTEM 2 THINKING
Irrational decisions	Rational decisions
Fast	Slow
Easy	Hard
Based on biases, stereotypes, perceptions	Based on facts, realties
Happens when alone, or with the herd, the mob	Happens in groups, tribal meetings
Fear driven, absence of trust	Trust driven, happens when trust exists

Evaluating System 1 can be useful as Kahneman points out in *Thinking, Fast and Slow*. It's what gets your foot to the brake when a truck blows the stop sign at a busy intersection. It's the thinking that puts you on guard when you hear a loud noise, and it supplies the answer when someone asks, what's 2 + 2? It is also the kind of thinking that protects the status quo, rejects new ideas and methods, and makes people more likely to act in order to avert a loss than to achieve a gain. System 1 is the realm of habit and stereotype. Of particular interest to us, Kahneman argues that System 1 thinking tends to substitute an easier question for a more difficult one whenever it can. Bluntly, it is lazy and often absolutely wrong when it thinks it is right.

System 2 thinking is complex and difficult. It requires stepping back, rising above the processes in place at an organization, and deliberating about things that might be taken for granted or rarely considered. Our stereotypes and biases are mental shortcuts that are lazy, requiring no patience. We should not be surprised that they guide so much decision-making—often under the guise of rational thought—since they avoid the difficult work of true analysis and deliberation.

Thanks to Kahneman, we could alter the Henry Ford quote I included in Part I to read, "*System 2* thinking is the hardest work there is, which is the probable reason why so few people engage in it." Everyone in your organization is thinking throughout the day, but a surprising amount of that thought is lazy, impatient, uninformed System 1 thinking.

The Seven Questions demand System 2 thinking. They are tough, not lazy or based on biases. They might seem simple on their face, but getting to and maintaining *yes* on all of them is difficult, and at times, painful work. Creating *yes* on the answers to, *Do I belong?* as I've pointed out, means reflecting deeply about the core values on which the entire organization stands and defining every position before asking team members to reflect on whether or not their values fit the organization's and if their skills are adequate for their positions. It does not allow the substitution of an easier question, a hallmark of System 1 thinking.

The Seven Questions require patience and encourage us to use our "big brain" for System 2 thinking, but they also acknowledge the primal "little brain" responsible for System 1 thinking and protect against its tyranny. Humans evolved as tribal animals and for most of our history we were potential prey. We have a strong fight-or-flight response and are acutely attuned to how we fit into the tribe, since as social animals, our survival has depended on it.

The little brain is all about fear and non-acceptance. It evolved over millions of years, and it takes control when fears, threats, and uncertainty put us on the defensive. Patience and deliberation disappear when team members are led by the little brain's System 1 thinking. During a retreat at the Edward Lowe Foundation, Dino

Signore turned me on to the work of David Rock, who has worked on the application of neuroscience to leadership, published a helpful neurological model, which I'll introduce briefly here, since it will come up in later examples and help me form a clear context in as few words as possible.

Every new encounter, Rock argues, activates the little brain, which wants to avoid danger and gain reward. A new assignment or new team member at work is no different than a movement in the bush or a shadow at the mouth of the cave was for our forebears. Neurons are activated and hormones are released as we assess whether an event represents an opportunity for reward or a threat. As soon as we sense danger, the fight-or-flight response kicks in and the little brain takes charge.[11]

The threat response is powerful. Rock cites research showing that our perceptions of the way others treat us trigger the same primal neural responses that drive us toward food and away from predators, and experiments suggest that feelings of being rejected socially provoked the same brain activity as physical pain.[12] The threat response diverts oxygen and glucose from other parts of the brain, making analysis and problem-solving difficult just when it's needed most.

The reward response, on the other hand, allows the little brain to stand down and makes space for more-sophisticated System 2 thinking. Rock has identified the five qualities that activate the basic reward and threat circuitry in the brain. He uses the helpful acronym SCARF to describe this dynamic:

---

11   David Rock, "Managing with the Brain in Mind," strategy+business, August
      27, 2009, https://www.strategy-business.com/article/09306?gko=5df7f

12   Ibid.

S Status concerns our relative importance to others.

C Certainty is the degree to which we can predict the future.

A Autonomy is our sense of control over decisions in our work and lives.

R Relatedness is the degree of trust and empathy we feel with others.

F Fairness is the perception of impartial, just treatment.

Picture, as Rock says, something comfy, warm, and protective wrapped around the head and neck, and you'll get the idea of SCARF for team members.

Leaders who pay attention to these five qualities can minimize the threat response of the little brain and maximize the reward response. When people feel that their status is secure, they have an idea of what's coming, they have some control over decisions, they trust those they work with, and they are treated fairly, they have the security to engage in more-sophisticated thinking and analysis. Remember the people I described in Part I who my friend Paul McKee calls "busy fools," constantly rushing around, with no patience and no time to think? That sort of siege mentality often stems from an organizational culture that does not meet members' SCARF needs and unwittingly encourages System 1 thinking.

> I'LL ALSO USE SCARF AS A VERB THROUGHOUT—*TO SCARF*, IN A NEGATIVE CONNOTATION, IS TO TRIGGER A THREAT RESPONSE BY DIMINISHING SOMEONE'S STATUS, CERTAINTY, AUTONOMY, RELATEDNESS, OR FAIRNESS.

I'm a fan of the SCARF model because first of all, the physiological piece of it makes perfect sense to anyone who has watched a team member wither under a harsh performance review, get micromanaged, or suffer a blistering attack in a meeting. We have all seen people "get SCARFed," and nothing destroys trust and motivation faster.

I'll also use SCARF as a verb throughout—*to SCARF*, in a negative connotation, is to trigger a threat response by diminishing someone's Status, Certainty, Autonomy, Relatedness, or Fairness.

The other reason I like SCARF is that it dovetails perfectly with the Seven Questions. The question *Do I belong?* has everything to do with feeling comfortable in terms of status, certainty, and relatedness. Fairness is only possible if you understand and embrace what you are accountable for, how your work is measured, and how you are heard. I'll come back to SCARF and make more connections as we explore the Seven Questions because it's a helpful model at times, but I want to stress that if you are getting to *yes* on all of the Seven Questions, you're meeting the needs of SCARF too.

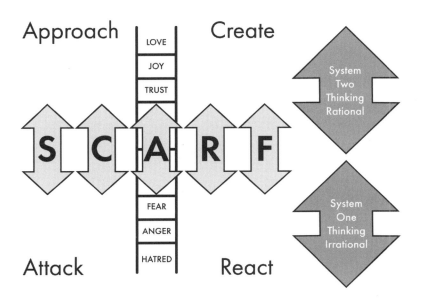

CHAPTER 5

HOW FAR ARE YOU FROM ATTAINING AND MAINTAINING *YES* TO THE 7QS?

OKAY, ENOUGH ABOUT neuroscience and behavioral economics. Almost. This, as I've said, is not one of those books with a 20,000-foot view. It is designed to be a manual for the trenches—practical and hands-on. I will confess that as a student of human behavior, I'm endlessly fascinated by the evolutionary and biological roots of what I do. I often refer to myself as a "tribes" person, because the dynamics of any organization are essentially tribal. I'm intrigued by the role of the little brain in decision-making, and I do think that leaders who are interested can benefit from some knowledge of Daniel Kahneman's ideas.

In the rest of this Part, I will explore what each question entails, its benefits, why it works, where organizations tend to fall short, and how answering *yes* builds patience. The order of the questions is no accident. The first two—*Do I belong?* and *Do I believe?*—are foundational and by far the most important. The next three: *Am I accountable? Am I measured well?* and *Is my opinion heard?* are primarily about communication and return us to the point of precise language. They involve everything from reflecting on how meetings are named and structured, to clearly stating the purpose of the organization.

The last two questions, about *development* and *balance*, involve everyone's favorite internal radio station, WIIFM—What's In It For Me? These questions are vital for buy-in, loyalty, and engagement. They help team members who can get to *yes* see that their values and goals align with the organization's.

Each question has two parts. The organization must answer the first part before it can prompt team members to ask themselves the second. I'll give concrete examples along the way and explore the effects of not attaining *yes*. Our exploration of each question in Part II ends with an exercise, Diagnosing Patience, which will help you to assess just how close to *yes* your organization already is.

The Seven Questions are intimately intertwined and overlap in many ways. Team members can't agree with how they're being measured (Question 4), for instance, if they don't know what they're accountable for (Question 3). It's easier to determine if you have or can develop the skills your position requires, as Question 1 asks, or if you have a sense of your development path within the organization, covered in Question 6.

Answering the Seven Questions is an ongoing process, not one and done, as I'll demonstrate in Part III, "Attaining and Maintaining *Yes*." The first step in becoming a Patient Organization, though, involves building an awareness of the kinds of gaps I began Part II talking about: How patient is your organization? How far are you from *yes* on each question? The rest of Part II will point you toward the answers you already have.

Do I Belong?

Yes means...

> **Organization:** *We have clearly defined our core values, positions, and all skills need for our positions.*

> **Team member:** *I fit the organization's core values, and I have or can develop the skills my positions demand.*

WHY IS THIS question the first and most important of the Seven Questions? Well, I began this book by talking about the dream behind the birth of every organization. The heart of that dream rests with the people that entrepreneurs envision surrounding themselves with, and stuffed into the gap between the dream and the soulless machine it so often becomes are people who don't belong, the wedges breaking our organization apart.

Again, nothing sucks more energy from an organization or destroys patience faster than people who do not belong. Entrepreneurs don't imagine collecting such people, but they creep in over time and in the worst instances, become organizational terrorists, holding hostage the team members who belong (more on that later). Answering *yes* to this question is the most important step in becoming a Patient Organization.

My father had it right: "If it wasn't for the people, it would be easy." He would say this with a twinkle in his eye, and a wry smile before digging back into the hard work that involves people. People aren't just the biggest source of problems; as I said in Part I, at the core, *every problem* at an organization is a people problem.

For both the organization as a whole and individual team members, attaining and maintaining *yes* on the question *Do I belong?* takes serious work, but the payoff is hard to overestimate. If every problem is, at bottom, a people problem, think of the enormous number of problems that get solved or prevented simply by having people who belong. Doing the difficult work of maintaining *yes* on this question has exponential benefits, creating a snowball effect that lets you roll right over the competition.

This question also tops the list because it addresses one of our most fundamental needs as humans, right up there with finding food and avoiding danger. We evolved as tribal creatures, and the need to belong is powerful because for millions of years our lives depended on it. As I mentioned, David Rock's research suggests that social situations—a meeting, performance review, presentation—can trigger the same primal threat response as an attacking bear.

Sadly, those who don't belong can live with the threat response almost continually activated, as they get SCARFed again and again and fall back into System 1 thinking. Those who do belong are comfortable with their status, certainty, autonomy, and relatedness, and believe they are treated with fairness. This gives them the security and confidence to analyze honestly, take risks, think creatively, admit mistakes, and be friendly with fellow team members, even during fierce debate. They are free to engage in System 2 thinking. In Part III, I will help you assess whether or not your OOS actively attracts those who can maintain *yes* and repels those who can't.

Team members who attain a *yes* answer to the question *Do I belong?* are patient, and they contribute to deep reserves of patience in the organization. They are patient with fellow team members because they aren't worried about their status, certainty, and related-ness. They are patient with leaders because they feel good about the levels of fairness and autonomy they're being shown. And if they are getting to and maintaining *yes* on the rest of the Seven Questions too, then they are able to take the long view and think deeply about problems and goals.

Recall our discussion of leadership and management in Part I. Management is about daily needs—sales numbers, new equipment, filling a missed order—and working *in* the business, as Michael Gerber, author of *The E-Myth,* says. Leadership is about the big picture, strategy, and working *on* the business. Those who don't belong must be managed. They spend their days scratching items off the never-ending to-do list that managers feed them. Managing is difficult, time-consuming, and impossible to scale.

Team members who belong can be led. They are given a task, and then they ask a couple clarifying questions and complete it without oversight. As soon as they do, they're back, saying not only, "Hey, what's next?" but also, "I was thinking about this." People who belong and who are led share in the burden and excitement of higher-level thinking with leaders, and free up the leadership team to do even more work *on* the business, to stick with Gerber's model, instead of simply *in* it.

People who belong are also just more fun to be around. Let's face it, no one wants to be around jerks. People don't start businesses in order to surround themselves with bozos, yet this is the single biggest problem at most organizations, even if it's framed in other ways: *they're all people problems.* So how does it happen, this prolifera-tion of jerks?

It's tempting to blame the jerks—many leaders do—but it's not their fault that they're embedded in your organization. In fact, the jerks often aren't even jerks. The problem is that the organization often has not done the hard work of defining positions and skills clearly, so what *yes* means to the question *Do I belong?* is unclear. One leaders or one department's jerk can be another's A-player. Is it the square jerk's fault he wound up in a round position hole? The process starts with leaders finding clarity on values, positions, and skills.

Before team members can be prompted to ask themselves *Do I belong?* leaders must decide on the organization's core values. As I said at the start of Part II, the core values are there. You have the answers, but they are usually buried. In Part III, I'll talk about Patrick Lencioni's methods for unearthing and developing your organization's core values. Maybe you feel that your core values are already clear and well integrated into the organization. That might be the case, but in my experience, that is exceedingly rare. There's a reason you're reading this book. At the end of this section, our Diagnosing Patience exercise will help you reflect on your OOS, asking if it helps you to determine how strong your core values are and how far your organization is from enjoying *yes* on the first of the Seven Questions.

The Diagnosing Patience exercise will also help you assess how well you have defined each position within the organization—the second key task leaders and teams must complete before they can have team members ask themselves, *Do I belong?* For team members, the first half of this question prompts them to assess whether or not their values align with the organization's. The second part asks them to assess whether they have or can develop the skillsets necessary to fill their positions. Aligning with core values is vital, but a software developer who believes in the organization's values and can't write code is in the wrong position. A whiz-bang coder who doesn't buy the overall values can't adequately fill the position, either.

You'll note that I use "positions" rather than "jobs," "hats," or Jim Collins's increasingly popular "seats" to refer to the various roles in an organization. Like saying "team member," over employee. The term "positions" originated with my sports and sailing experience, but after decades of running my own companies and coaching others, I have come to realize it's the most accurate label. A "job" is actually made up of many positions. On offense, I play center and report to the offensive-line coach, while on defense I play linebacker and report to the defensive-back coach. Marketing director is a job label, sure, but at a particular organization, it might include a creative position, a supervisory/mentor position, a client services position, a copy editor position, and so on.

Team members need to know the purpose and requirements of each position, a more complex and accurate construct in my view than the simple term "job" indicates. Speaking of views, I also like "position" because it implies attitude and belief, a particular stance. *What's your position on this issue?* we ask. Since it's my contention that an organization is a fiction resting entirely on the belief of its members, this connotation of "position" is not just a linguistic trick. It is existential, central to what it means to belong and to believe and, in a very real sense, to create an organization

THIS CONNOTATION OF "POSITION" IS NOT JUST A LINGUISTIC TRICK. IT IS EXISTENTIAL, CENTRAL TO WHAT IT MEANS TO BELONG AND TO BELIEVE AND, IN A VERY REAL SENSE, TO CREATE AN ORGANIZATION ANEW EACH DAY. "POSITION" IMPLIES THAT EVERY TEAM MEMBER, FROM THE JANITOR TO THE CEO PLAYS A VITAL ROLE IN THE ORGANIZATION'S SURVIVAL.

anew each day. "Position" implies that every team member, from the janitor to the CEO plays a vital role in the organization's survival.

Each position has a particular perspective, and when two positions look at something, you can determine where that something truly lies. In navigation, we call this *triangulation*: you look at something and you have a position, or a bearing, and somebody else looks at it, and he or she has another bearing, and together, you can get a precise fix on that thing.

Triangulation

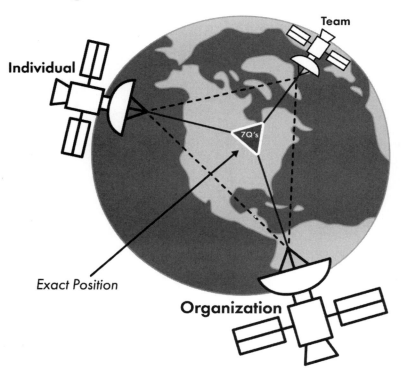

Many of the owners and leadership teams I run into *think* they have already done their share of the work on the first of our Seven Questions and accounted for every position in the organization.

They have job descriptions from HR, titles, and a classic, direct-report org chart. None of this gets you to a solid *yes*. None of this deals with positions. I'll help you test if your OOS is providing the concrete steps for you to get there in terms of both belonging and accountability in Part III, but the process begins with assessing all of the organization's needs. Forget about titles and jobs and think about everything that must be thought about and done every second of every day. What positions emerge from that exercise? Where's the overlap? What are the gaps? The organization must engage in this process before leaders can ask team members if they belong.

The organization that attains and maintains *yes* on *Do I belong?* has an incredible gatekeeper for building and maintaining a Patient Organization. Every position is clear, and the core values it has defined can then be used in recruiting, interviewing, training, measuring, and developing team members. Those core values become an integral part of the decision rubrics that every Patient Organization builds into the system. *Of these three difficult options, which aligns best with our core values?*

When people problems arise, *Do I belong?* also becomes part of an invaluable checklist, along with the rest of the Seven Questions. There's a problem with Dave? Well, *does he belong? Does he believe? What exactly is Dave accountable for and does he understand it? Is he being measured well? Has he embraced the agreed metrics?* You get the idea. *Do I belong?* not only becomes the gatekeeper for hiring new people via the tools of an effective OOS, but it also makes the difficult conversations down the road much easier because team members have been kept in the loop about core values, purpose, accountability, measurement, etc., and have been actively involved in asking the key questions related to them.

I keep talking about hard work, and attaining and maintaining *yes* on the Seven Questions requires plenty, but when coupled with a consistent OOS, this work saves immense amounts of time and work. Once you have established core values and defined every position, the process of maintaining *yes* can start to feel magical because your people pick it up and keep it going. Gaps are filled and duplication is eliminated as things begin to fall in place. Oftentimes people who don't belong self-select out of the organization once they're presented with clear core values and well-defined positions, saving leaders headaches and tough conversations.

Getting to *yes* on *Do I belong?* is also *the* key to growth. A client of mine, Sine Tea, provides a good example. The company started small and from the start, made *education* and *sustainability* priorities, alongside *profits*. Partners Bob and Alan were successful and had a completely open-door policy, but as the organization approached two hundred employees and expanded nationally, growth took its toll.

Expansion and quality appeared contradictory, as did growth and inclusiveness, sustainability and education. Don, the star salesman, wasn't cutting it as a National Sales Director. Russell, who had done a great job packing tea, couldn't stay off the line now that he was Operations Manager. It was hard to tell if Katrina, the vice president of culture and sustainability, did a good job because when the team and I forgot about titles and began defining positions, no one knew what she was accountable for. Alan left the organization, and since every driver, packer, and admin still had Bob's ear, he was wearing thin.

Attaining and maintaining *yes* on *Do I belong?* took care of many of Sine Tea's growing pains, and it did so without acrimony. Within nine months, some employees who couldn't *align to yes* self-selected out. Faced with the organization's core values and defined positions, Katrina realized her deepest values involved the industry. She happily went to work for a trade association, and the organization did not need to replace a fancy title that had no real accountabilities—a job title without positions. Other team members stayed but realized they did not belong in their current positions. Don, for instance, voluntarily moved back to direct sales, where he was much happier and could wholeheartedly get to *yes* on belonging. With a leadership team that belonged and greater autonomy, Bob could preserve his sanity and spend more time working *on* the business, rather than just *in* it.

Becoming a Patient Organization gave Sine Tea the ability to maintain consistency and quality during its expansion, and it all started with getting to and maintaining *yes* on the question, *Do I belong?*

DIAGNOSING PATIENCE

DO I BELONG?

Follow the prompts below, then at the end, after you have answered all of the prompts, rate how close your organization is to attaining and maintaining *yes* on this question by circling one:

FAR AWAY   MANY MILES   RIGHT AROUND THE CORNER   THERE

Grab a piece of paper and follow these prompts:

PROMPTS

1.   Write down your organization's core values.

2.   Are the things you wrote down presented systematically during interviewing, training, onboarding, etc., as "core values?"

3.   Write down one time during the last two days that you anchored a decision in the organization's core values and framed it to team members using that term.

4.   Has your leadership team in the last six months assessed everything that needs to be thought about and accomplished at your organization?

5.   Are you engaging team members to ask if they have the needed skills for those positions at least every ninety days?

6.   Has all overlap been eliminated and have all gaps been filled on your list of positions?

Review your answers using my highly unscientific key, on the next page—and don't fudge. Remember, you're the one with the answers, and you probably know in your gut, without reading another word, how far you are from *yes*.

KEY

1. If initially answering Prompt 1 took more than ninety seconds, you rate **FAR AWAY**.

    > More than five things noted? That's a laundry list, not core values—**MANY MILES**.

    > Only one or two things noted? That's sketchy—**FAR AWAY**.

    > If the language is not clear, simple, and specific (each item ranging from one strong word to a basic sentence), you can probably tell where you stand between **FAR AWAY** and **RIGHT AROUND THE CORNER,** but There, you ain't.

2. If you initially answered *no* to Prompt 2, you're somewhere between **FAR AWAY** and **MANY MILES**. If you answered *yes*, you might be **THERE** or **RIGHT AROUND THE CORNER**.

3. If you initially couldn't answer Prompt 3, you're somewhere between **FAR AWAY** and **MANY MILES**. If you could, you're probably either **THERE** or **RIGHT AROUND THE CORNER.**

4. If you initially answered *no* to Prompt 4, you're **FAR AWAY**. If you answered *yes*, you're probably **THERE** or **RIGHT AROUND THE CORNER.**

5. If you initially answered *no* to Prompt 5, you're **FAR AWAY**. If you answered *yes*, you're somewhere between **THERE** and **MANY MILES**.

6. If you initially answered *yes* to Prompt 6, you're **THERE**—and probably lying. If it's close, you're somewhere between **FAR AWAY** and **RIGHT AROUND THE CORNER.**

Do I Believe?

Yes means...

> **Organization:** *We know our why; it keeps us focused and allows us to have a clearly laid out strategy for achieving it.*

> **Team member:** *I believe in our why and leadership's strategy for achieving it. I get Simon Sineck's "Golden Circle"—the why, the how, and the what of my organization.*

THE SECOND OF the Seven Questions is as important as the first. If, as I have argued, an organization is a fiction, a shared belief created by team members, then harboring people who can't get to *yes* on the question *Do I believe?* obviously does serious damage. Harbor enough of them, and the organization ceases to exist.

Nonprofits get this. They often have issues with position clarity and attack strategy when it comes to executing their purpose, or *why*, but they tend to understand that the organization's overall mission is important, driving loyalty, productivity, and cohesion. They use it to recruit and to interview and to fire up the troops. They know their *why* is the reason so many talented, motivated people eschew higher pay and benefits to work in the nonprofit world. Team members who care deeply about the environment, social justice, inequality, animal rights—pick a cause—are willing to work long and hard for less pay and fewer benefits because they believe in a particular *why*.

Is there a better way to motivate and focus a team than to highlight to members the greater good they're striving for? Executive directors at nonprofits say *no* without hesitation, but I'm always amazed by the number of PBOs (Private Business Owners) who have not given their *why* much thought, articulated it clearly, or communicated it to the troops.

Some answer my question above—what better way to motivate and focus?—with a single word: *Money*. To which I say, *really?* Is that what you want on your tombstone? *He/she made a lot of money.* Is that really what gets you out of bed in the morning or keeps you at the office until midnight when you're immersed in an important project? I ask this as someone who fully understands and appreciates the value of a buck. I started and ran four companies and was driven to make money at all of them. I've spent the last decade coaching leadership teams on strategies that make them more money, but extra money is a motivator only to the extent that it's critical to peoples' perception of their imagined futures. Beyond that, a sole focus on money conveys that you actually don't give a flip about them or where their lives are going. (Question 6 on development and the Daniel Pink book, *Drive,* offer additional insight on the subject.)

The point is, no matter how important making money is, the *why* is more important for most of your team members. Was Steve Jobs motivated by money? He certainly made his share, and I'm sure that pleased him, but money wasn't his main motivator. He returned to Apple in 1997 after the company recorded a quarterly loss of $708 million and brought back the *why*—and what a difference that made. He was driven to revolutionize the way people interacted with technology, to provide superior design and a user experience like no other. That was his *why*, and perhaps, because it was so strong, he proved a master at using narrative and gestures both grand and small to motivate his team around a purpose, as well as his strategy for getting there.

Okay, you might think, "the organizational *why* has been a big factor at Apple, where genius developers and designers are working on the next iGadget—but can my team accomplish this? Can we attain a similar purpose and belief?" Yes, your team can. One of my clients has this belief statement: *We believe in the power of listening.* What are they, lawyers, counselors, music producers? No, this is a janitorial supplies distributor. They believe they are a customer-facing organization every single day and that they find their competitive advantage by truly taking the time to listen to their customers, vendors, and the market. Before they put anything in place, they ask, "Will that make us better listeners?" And while janitorial supplies might seem unglamorous, team members see this mission as a source of pride and loyalty.

I'll give more examples of belief statements and the organizational *why* in Part III when I explore strategies for using your OOS to get to *yes* on this question, but other good ones from my clients include: *Relationships that last forever; Improving the way people make and use energy;* and *Empowering others to accomplish that which they never thought they could.* Each of these organizations learned to motivate team members and shape strategy by getting to *yes* on the question, *Do I believe?*

Still skeptical? Recall the Gallup stats I cited in Part I, showing that 70 percent of all US workers are either neutrally engaged or unengaged at work. Here's another: "Only slightly more than a third of millennial workers strongly agree that the mission or purpose of their organization makes them feel their job is important," according to Gallup. But focusing on the *why* turns the numbers upside down: 67 percent of millennials are engaged at work "when they strongly agree that the mission or purpose of their company makes them feel their job is important." Only 14 percent of millennials who strongly disagree with that statement are engaged. Think about that math. Millennials are nearly *five times* more likely to be engaged when the organization has a strong *why* they can connect their work to.

Those stats are worth considering, since millennials are nearly 40 percent of the workforce as I write this, and could account for as much as 75 percent by 2025—but as I pointed out in Part I, this is not just about millennials. They might have a little more patience in pursuing purpose than do previous generations, but all team members want to feel attached to a *why* that makes their days at an organization mean something. The desire to be part of some larger purpose is embedded in our DNA, an integral part of what it means to be human. I won't belabor the point, since I've made it elsewhere, but this also stems from our evolutionary and tribal roots. Working together for some greater good—hunting a buffalo or cleaning out a cave—was how we survived. The bigger *why* connects us to the tribe, helps address SCARF, and allows us to align personal purpose with organizational purpose.

I don't mean to suggest that focusing on the *why* is about self-sacrifice. Just the opposite. Paradoxically, a selfish, personal need is met by focusing on the larger organizational *why*. I have coached football players for years because I think it builds character and confidence and teaches important skills to the young men on my teams, of course, but I also take great personal satisfaction from it. Serving that greater good lets me tune in to WIIFM—What's In It For Me—like nothing else.

As I said, this question is just as important as *Do I belong?* and like that first one, the benefits of getting to *yes* here are immense. Gallup data show that when workers are driven by the larger mission, "companies realize major performance gains, including increased employee loyalty and retention, greater customer engagement, improved strategic alignment and enhanced clarity about work priorities."

When *why* is clearly articulated and integrated throughout the organization, your *why* allows you to focus and engage in clear System 2 thinking as you allocate limited resources. Like the first question, *Do I belong?*, this one becomes a litmus test and a key part of a Patient Organization's built-in decision matrices. *We're faced with two difficult options here? Okay, which one will best serve our purpose?* A true *why* allows you to simplify and focus, to choose to decide to say firmly *no*.

When I turned my sailing gear catalogue into the dotcom, Layline.com, our purpose stayed the same. It was taking care of the finite days our customers had on the water and protecting their weekends. We were dealing with clients who were passionate about their sailboat racing but very busy, with limited time on the water. We saw their weekends as sacred because of our *why* (weekend days = finite), and so we never considered putting off a call or delivery of the best equipment until Monday. There was no question about it—call them, ship it overnight, don't worry about the cost, protect the weekend.

As we found at Layline, having a *why* allows you to debate and argue patiently about the *what* and the *how*. Our purpose percolated through daily operations and shaped our work week. Because we believed in freedom for sailors, we protected their Fridays by delivering the right things on time to the right place. We would include screws and caulk, so they would not have to make a trip to the hardware store, and send articles with their packages so they could study and use their gear to its full potential, all without being asked, which meant listening, asking questions, planning ahead, and working a little harder on Thursdays. The *why* wasn't just part of a logo or mentioned annually at a retreat. We integrated it fully into our daily work.

Knowing and leading with the *why* builds patience and allows the big picture to be contemplated. Keeping one eye always on the overall mission means slowing down to work on broader strategy as well as daily needs—*on*, and not just *in*, the organization.

I hope I've made the case for why *why* is important, but I want to caution that I'm talking about a true, authentic purpose here. Your *why* can't simply be something posted on the wall, a plaque, or platitude. Your "mission statement," I'm sorry to inform you, probably doesn't cut it. In Part III, I'll talk in detail about the concrete steps to using your OOS to develop your *why*—one simple fundamental sentence. Once it's been decided, the language carefully crafted and agreed on, it must be truly integrated throughout the organization via your OOS.

The second half of getting to *yes* on *Do I believe?* involves strategy. A *why* is meaningless if the organization does not develop and communicate a strategy for fulfilling it. Team members must get to *yes* on the strategy as well as the purpose. Those who like the destination but not the route should find their own way—to the exit. Nonprofits, as I mentioned, are often good at getting team members to *yes* on the *why*, but they often suffer severely from lack of buy-in on the chosen strategy for getting there.

If faith as small as a mustard seed can move a mountain, imagine what an entire team of people who feel strongly that they belong and wholeheartedly believe in the mission can accomplish at your organization.

DO I BELIEVE?

Follow the prompts below, then at the end, after you have answered all of the prompts, rate how close your organization is to attaining and maintaining *yes* on this question by circling one:

FAR AWAY   MANY MILES   RIGHT AROUND THE CORNER   THERE

Grab a piece of paper and follow these prompts:

PROMPTS

1. Write down your organization's purpose, its why, in a belief statement.

2. Find three random members of the team—one senior leader, one mid-level person, and someone on the frontline—and ask, what is the purpose of our organization? Write down their answers.

3. When did you last use your why—the specific language noted in number 1 above—to arrive at a decision with team members or as a reference point in a meeting?

Review your answers using my highly unscientific key, on the next page—and don't fudge. Remember, you're the one with the answers, and you probably know in your gut, without reading another word, how far you are from *yes*.

KEY

1. If your initial answer to Prompt 1 was more than one sentence, you're either at **FAR AWAY** or **MANY MILES**.

2. Could your initial statement be put in this form: *We believe **in the power of** _____?* If not, you're somewhere between **FAR AWAY** and **RIGHT AROUND THE CORNER**, not **THERE**.

3. Could your initial statement be used to say *no,* to focus, to simplify? If not, you're **FAR AWAY**.

4. If the three random members of the team answered substantially the same for Prompt 2, you're **THERE**.

5. If your initial answer to Prompt 3 is more than two days out, you're somewhere between **FAR AWAY** and **MANY MILES**.

Am I Accountable?

Yes means...

> **Organization:** *We have done the hard work as an organization to be sure our accountability, responsibility, and position structure is clear.*

> **Team member:** *I understand and embrace the purpose of my positions and what I should be thinking about and doing in each.*

TITLES ARE THE perfect example of System 1 thinking, lazy, unclear, and I think they suck the energy out of organizations.

I dislike them very much. They're like giant blankets that obscure thought and action with their flat bulk. People who don't belong or believe often hide behind them, clinging like infants to those hollow labels for comfort and security.

Sure, we need legal titles to enter into contracts, but to describe a position or group of positions as Chief This or Vice That often muddies the waters rather than adding clarity.

Leaders, though, are reluctant to admit the inadequacies of titles. Many owners and leadership teams I work with recognize pretty quickly that their organizations have not gotten to *yes* on belonging and believing, but they think they're doing just fine in getting team members to understand and embrace what they are accountable for. "Look at this organizational chart," they say. "It's all right here. Alex, the marketing assistant, reports to Debbie, the marketing manager, who reports to Susan, the marketing director, who reports to Victor, the VP of marketing, who reports to Chuck, the COO, who reports to Sally, the CEO . . ."

Sorry, but that is not true accountability. "Put that chart and all titles aside for now," I tell them, and then say, "let's think about everything—I mean *everything*—that needs to be done in this organization, every quarter, month, week, day, minute, and second. For example, if you're a construction company, you've got to be thinking about safety every second—no lapses." *Yes* on accountability means honestly assessing all of the thinking and doing that must take place at an organization and then matching people with the inventory of thinking and doing *positions* that emerge from this exercise.

In Part III, as we work on attaining *yes,* I'll talk about the first *yeses* and a process that is not easy or comfortable for team members, but here, I want to emphasize that "jobs" and "titles" are blunt instruments. Anyone who has worked at a big corporation knows that vice presidents can propagate like rabbits. Vice President of Operations, Vice President of Sustainability, Vice President of Parking. . . . What do these people *do? It's unclear* and *not much* are two dismayingly frequent answers.

Thinking in terms of "position" clarifies the discussion. Each job contains many positions, and they shift over time. Some positions are purely about *thinking.* Some are purely *doing.* In my coaching and in these pages, I draw a distinction between "accountability" and "responsibility." You are *accountable* for thinking—planning, considering, assessing a decisions' potential impact. You are *responsible* for doing—executing, producing. Agreeing on these terms allows leaders and team members to clarify accountabilities and responsibilities.

Do you understand and embrace both what you are accountable for thinking about and responsible for doing?

Many positions are a combination of thinking and doing, but organizations typically don't do the vital work of communicating how much time team members should be spending on each. Just considering the large number of positions at even small organizations, as well as how much thinking and doing is attached to each one, requires patience—doing the hard work your competition is unwilling to do. It is *so* much easier for them to be lazy, live in System 1 thinking, and hope that the titles on a direct-report/org chart are good enough.

Recall the client I talked about earlier, Sine Tea, which brought me in as the company's expansion caused growing pains. Katrina, the vice president of culture and sustainability, had an impressive title and a high-paying job, but when we started talking about actual *positions*, no one could point to what a vice president of culture did. Sustainability was at the root of their *why* and everyone was a part of that effort; sustainability was part of every position, so there was no need for a VP of that. Team members didn't know what Katrina was really supposed to be thinking about and doing.

Everyone assumed that Sine's CFO performed the usual array of tasks that people attach to that title, but when we drilled down into actual positions involving finance, it turned out that Bob, the owner, who had a strong financial background, loved the work and was filling many of the finance positions. He was good at these positions and, frankly, did not want to give them up. So, the clear answer was that the CFO could go, and a wonderful controller and financial reporting person could be hired to fill the positions that the CEO/owner did not want to fill. Sine Tea had a typical org chart and the usual roster of titles, but these only distracted leadership from the overlap and gaps, as well as a number of org chart jobs that lacked purpose.

Titles are rarely descriptive enough, and forgive me for beating this drum again, but language matters. If we're not naming things accurately and consistently—a problem, a position, a core value—it is clear we don't believe in the same things. That makes clarity impossible and allows dysfunction. It endangers the shared belief and meaning that is the organization.

A one-and-done effort at defining positions doesn't solve all the problems either, since team members typically have to switch between them, depending on needs. At most organizations, positions change with particular seasons. At Layline.com, the nature of the business made those changes stark. Sales would start in mid-March and turn off in September or October, depending on the hurricane season. The shifts from heavy selling to heavy planning to heavy web and catalog execution meant that a team member's positions might switch from phone work to vendor relations to buying to copy editing to photography.

Seasonal shifts in positions present challenges. Many humans, especially those engaged in System 1 lazy thinking, want to do the same thing every day. They seek familiarity and see it as a way to protect their certainty, autonomy, and other SCARF needs. Returning to my football analogy, I play center on offense and report to the offensive-line coach, but must switch to the linebacker position and report to the defensive-back coach when it's time to play defense. Leaders and team members must coordinate constantly to ensure that positions are being filled in smart ways amid seasonal changes. Taking the time to do that difficult work requires constant vigilance and patience.

The process of attaining and maintaining *yes* on accountabilities and responsibilities is a revelation for organizations. Team members often are not aware of the positions they're currently filling until their organization insists on patience analysis. We have all seen this at organizations we've been a part of. Someone jumps in to help out or pick up slack, and pretty soon another task becomes part of their job. The job and title remain the same, but a position has been added.

A client I recently worked with shared that an employee was returning from maternity leave. The organization has one hundred and eighty team members, and she was hired to work in her area of expertise, the benefits side of human resources—open enrollment, health plans, etc. Her return was a perfect time to peel back the lid and look at positions; it turned out that before she left, she had been spending a lot of time on payroll, accounts payable, and accounts receivable, certainly not her highest and best use. We used this opportunity to realign, and the team loved it. At another organization, a salesperson was spending significant time thinking about development of a new product—a thinking position—when he really didn't have the authority for that position or the know-how or experience it required.

I'll discuss in Part III, how clarifying positions helps all team members understand the purpose, domain, and authority of their "jobs" (a terrific model explained in the helpful book *Holacracy: The New Management System for a Rapidly Changing World*).[13] Those are the three key areas that tend to get cloudy and must be defined in order to enable *yes* and build patience.

Creating what a solid *yes* looks like on this question of *accountability* is an involved process, but the benefits are enormous. The frustrations and impatience that come with "position creep"—the insidious, unconsidered, ad hoc accretion of tasks, duties, and expec-

---

13 Brian J. Robertson, *Holacracy: The New Management System for a Rapidly Changing World* (New York: Henry Holt and Company, 2015).

tations—tends to hurt the team members who belong and believe the most: the engaged. The engaged are the ones who jump in when someone's on leave, stay late when it's crunch time, and pick up the ball someone else dropped. Over time, they can become uncertain about what they're really accountable for, or can no longer embrace it. Their primary positions, the things they're best at and were hired for, might suffer as positions quietly morph. We are in the danger zone with these folks because the organizations OOS is not maintaining clear accountability.

Team members seek to answer *yes* on this question because not understanding or embracing what they're accountable for is one of the biggest sources of frustration at organizations. This is where clarity disappears. Accountability ties back closely to SCARF. Those who belong and believe can't feel secure in terms of SCARF if they don't fully understand what they're accountable for. Hazy positions mean they have less certainty about what they will be thinking and doing in any given week. If they're taking over others' duties or being diverted from their own, relatedness and fairness suffer. Their sense of autonomy, a precondition for accountability, suffers. And all of this together can damage their status within the organization.

Accountability must be addressed in conjunction with measurement, which is the focus of our next question.

AM I ACCOUNTABLE?

Follow the prompts below, then at the end, after you have answered all of the prompts, rate how close your organization is to attaining and maintaining *yes* on this question by circling one:

FAR AWAY   MANY MILES   RIGHT AROUND THE CORNER   THERE

Grab a piece of paper and follow these prompts:

PROMPTS

1.   Have you inventoried everything that must be thought about and done at the organization and defined which employees are filling which *positions* (not just "jobs")?

2.   When was the last time you discussed with a team member the amount of thinking versus doing he or she should engage in for a particular position?

3.   Do all "titles" at the organization accurately reflect the positions within their domain?

4.   When was the last time something important did not get done because team members were not sure who was responsible for it?

Review your answers using my highly unscientific key, on the next page—and don't fudge. Remember, you're the one with the answers, and you probably know in your gut, without reading another word, how far you are from *yes*.

KEY

5. If you initially answered *no to* Prompt 1, you're **FAR AWAY**. If you answered *yes,* you're somewhere between **RIGHT AROUND THE CORNER** and **THERE**.

6. If your initial answer to Prompt 2 is more than a week or two, you're **MANY MILES** away. More than that and you're **FAR AWAY**.

7. If you initially answered *no* to Prompt 3, you're not alone, but you are somewhere between **FAR AWAY** and **RIGHT AROUND THE CORNER**.

8. If your initial answer to Prompt 4 is less than a month, you're somewhere between **FAR AWAY** and **RIGHT AROUND THE CORNER**, but you probably are not **THERE**. If it was yesterday and the day before, you're likely **FAR AWAY**.

Am I Measured Well?

Yes means...

Organization: *We have agreed upon ways, including concrete numbers, to objectively measure all team members and allow them the autonomy to meet these metrics.*

Team member: *I understand and embrace how and why I am measured and know what constitutes "a good job."*

ALL OF THE Seven Questions are tightly interconnected, but perhaps none more so than Questions 3 and 4. An organization must define its positions and make sure that team members understand what they are accountable for and responsible for before it can measure performance, and without good ways to measure performance, there is no true accountability.

As I hope you appreciate by now, each "job" might include five, six, or seven positions, which may change according to the seasons of a particular industry. Organizations typically have broad measures of overall performance in place, but each of a team member's positions should have some sort of deliverable, a particular measure for that particular position. The same set of metrics won't work for all team members, obviously. What constitutes a good job for a salesperson, a truck driver, and an accountant varies widely. Leaders get this, but often fail to recognize that metrics should be attached to each position within a job (by "metrics," of course, I mean any means of measuring—some might have numbers attached and others be more subjective; red, yellow, green). Metrics paint the picture and allow employees to be accountable for their defined roles.

While I am not a pure mathematician—remember, I am slightly dyslexic and graduated with accounting and statistics degrees; yes, that is scary—I can see the numbers. I always tried to teach and coach so my folks could visualize what the numbers were "saying."

At Layline, one of our very first orientation items was a deep-dive into the nomenclature of margins. Margin in dollars, as a percent of gross, as net, as gross-margin return on investment—all sorts of good numbers that I wanted people to understand so we could have robust conversations and make rational decisions. These numbers were the bottom line language of Layline as an organization.

We were a catalog retailer and a dotcom, and we sold at shows and events—and each of these venues was a statistics honey-hole. We worked with SAS (Statistical Analysis Systems, the largest privately held software company on the planet) in the early days. My next-door neighbor was a VP there, and we were using the same beta software as Nations Bank to analyze our customer behavior and to predict future behavior. This wasn't backroom stuff. We brought it out to our frontline folks to help them understand why we were making decisions and how they could impact the results of our experiments. The numbers spoke to us.

Positive measures should build your team members' confidence in the decisions they make and the results they can achieve. This sort of measurement is a lot like setting up your sailboat for the upcoming race to go scorchingly fast. We can't see the wind, but we can see the things that impact our decisions. We can see, for instance, that the waves are just starting to form whitecaps, which means the wind is blowing between eight and ten knots. We can look at our compass and see the direction it's blowing and which way our boat will head. We can look at the clouds and make a prediction about where the wind, waves, and currents are headed. Using that data set, we can compare it to our "tune sheet" (which was our setup sheet) to choose if we'll use light-air, heavy-air, or medium-air equipment. That data tells us how tight to set the rig and the sails to go fast.

Just as we cannot see the wind when sailing, we can't see the future or into the minds of our customers in business either. We must collect and use data to make predictions. With awareness of this data, we can look to our "tune sheet" to be sure we are set up to achieve our ultimate goal.

A good measure set allows our people to see, discuss, and ultimately drive patient, repeatable results. A bad set can focus on long-term measurement at the expense of short-term metrics, or vice versa. As we'll explore in Part III, a strong Organizational Operating System will ensure that a good measurement has both long-term and short-term components. Whether the standard metrics are sales quotas, number of customers retained, or number of workers recruited, leaders must clearly communicate the endgame. *Here is our* why (that magical word again). *Here is what success looks like long-term and how your positions align with our overall purpose.* MBAs call these "long-term measures lagging indicators."

Leading indicators, much like their macroeconomic counterparts, measure activity along the way, as we move toward that endgame. Team members should think, here are the things I can work on, every day and every week, in pursuit of that larger goal. Here are the numbers that will let me know how well I'm progressing. Too often, leaders don't establish clear leading indicators with team members, or, worse, never have regular conversations around them.

Note that I said leaders should establish metrics *with* team members. When team members resist being measured and feel locked down or hampered by the process, that's often because it didn't include them. They might consider the metrics unfair or inaccurate. Giving them a voice in how they're measured can lead to creative and more accurate ways to track progress. Such conversations also give leaders a chance to explain why certain numbers are important to them and how the team member's positions relate to the overall goal. The metric that seemed unfair might get buy-in once leaders patiently explain their point of view. Having the conversation is key. Organizations that can't attain and maintain *yes* on the question *Am I measured well?* inevitably fall short on the next question, *Am I heard?*

Those who enjoy achieving *yes* when answering, *Am I measured well?* by establishing metrics with team members build a powerful sense of belonging and belief—the two foundations of the Seven Questions. Someone who is brought into the process no longer sees the agreed-on measurement as a leash or a limitation, but as a means to autonomy. It is fine to take away thoughts that these benchmarks have been reached and now it's up to you to pursue the goal. What sort of thinking and doing is necessary to hit these near and far targets?

I am not arguing for low standards or a free-for-all. The metrics must be agreed to by leaders and team members, and they must make sense for each position as well as the organization as a whole. But unless team members have a voice in how they're measured, they can't have real autonomy. Without autonomy, leaders can't lead—only manage. And management without leadership, as I've pointed out, is difficult, time consuming, and stunting for the organization.

Autonomy is at the heart of SCARF, and getting to *yes* on measurement is vital to meeting SCARF needs. Good metrics provide certainty and fairness, because team members know and have agreed on how they are measured. It's hard to say something you helped make and agreed to is unclear or unfair. If, on the other hand, the rules are always changing mid-game in a free-for-all, the primal threat response will kick in and System 1 irrational thinking will take over.

Objective, open metrics feed into team members' feelings of relatedness and status, too. People in similar positions are measured by similar numbers. They see how others are doing and exactly where they fit in the tribe. If they are doing a good job, their status is probably secure.

The process I'm describing takes—you guessed it—patience. Dropping a quota on someone from on high does not require collaboration, conversations, adjustments, or, frankly, much thinking. Neither do standard KPIs—the Key Performance Indicators found in every industry. While many might be useful, I'm generally not a fan of just accepting this type of measurement, because it's generic and not particular to the organization. If you are a lazy System 1 thinker, sure, go with the industry standard, the way everyone measures things—take it away. If you are a patient System 2 thinker, you will challenge the crap and come up with something your organization really believes. Blindly accepting KPIs just because is bad thinking.

A client who has more than sixty franchise hair salons is a good example of what I mean here. Their measure, up until this quarter, was the one espoused by the franchise: customer count. How many people are we getting in the door? Lately, they realized that the real riddle is haircutter retention. The organization's purpose is "joy through growth," and to fulfill it, they discovered, they must focus heavily on haircutter retention, an important driver of customer count. They now have a Haircutter Retention position with long-term and short-term metrics in place to achieve that goal. Retaining great hair cutters is job number one!

Performing the difficult work of creating such custom, collaborative metrics requires patience, but it builds patience, as well. It creates the focus and boundaries that patience demands. Team members can prioritize, and they learn to appreciate how even the most menial or painful short-term work is fulfilling a long-term purpose. They aren't wigging out on a regular basis, treating all work as equal, or focusing on the wrong stuff. Good measurement, you might say, is a kind of vaccine against Busy Fool Syndrome.

AM I MEASURED WELL?

Follow the prompts below, then at the end, after you have answered all of the prompts, rate how close your organization is to attaining and maintaining *yes* on this question by circling one:

FAR AWAY   MANY MILES   RIGHT AROUND THE CORNER   THERE

Grab a piece of paper and follow these prompts:

PROMPTS

1. Do all positions—not just jobs—have objective measures built in?

2. Do those measures include obtainable numbers, and both short-term and long-term components?

3. How often are senior leaders meeting with team members to get their input on and discuss metrics?

4. When is the last time you highlighted for team members the ways that their metrics connect to the organization's why?

Review your answers using my highly unscientific key, on the next page—and don't fudge. Remember, you're the one with the answers, and you probably know in your gut, without reading another word, how far you are from *yes*.

KEY

1. If you initially answered *no* to Prompt 1, you're **FAR AWAY**. If you answered *yes,* you might be somewhere between **RIGHT AROUND THE CORNER** and **THERE**.

2. If you initially answered *no* to Prompt 2, you're **FAR AWAY**. If you answered *yes,* you're somewhere between **RIGHT AROUND THE CORNER** and **THERE**.

3. If your initial answer to Prompt 3 was more than ninety days, you're **MANY MILES** or **FAR AWAY**. If it's ninety days or less, you might just be **THERE**.

4. If your initial answer to Prompt 4 was more than ninety days, you're **FAR AWAY**. If it's ninety days or less, you might just be **THERE**.

Am I Heard?

Yes means...

Organization: *We have clearly defined and followed communication channels to build trust and spur debate and problem-solving among team members.*

Team member: *I understand and embrace how I am heard and how my organization listens.*

EVEN EFFICIENT, FUNCTIONAL organizations with a clear purpose and strong core values tend to have meetings that live somewhere between poor and *please shoot me*. Meetings aren't the only way that opinions get heard in an organization, but they provide one of the most egregious examples of how leaders fall down when it comes to hearing team members.

Leaders with the patience to structure and use meetings effectively can create meetings that people not only find useful, but actually look forward to attending. Yes, I'm serious. Meetings tend to be handled so poorly that people can begin to think the terrain is naturally half-swamp. I completely disagree, but more on meetings later. First, I want to explore why it is so important that team members understand and embrace how they are heard. Those abysmal Gallup engagement stats I keep returning to rest at least partly on organizational deafness. We all want to be heard, and when we're not—whether it's at work, in a marriage, or as part of a club—we check out.

Communication, as I argued in Part I, is our unique gift as humans. It is our greatest example of and leap forward in intersubjectivity, the ability to share meaning. Once we learn to communicate through clear language, technology, religion, empires, and complex economies are born. Language is a vital part of our evolution, and whether the mechanism is the "talking stick" passed around the fire outside the hut or the weekly sales meeting, humans have a deep need to speak and be heard. Established channels of communication make us feel a part of the tribe and they fulfill our need for SCARF. The person who isn't heard begins to feel ostracized, which causes our primal threat response and System 1 thinking to rear their ugly heads.

It's a cliché, but effective communication really must be two-way. If leaders communicate their expectations, goals, and feedback, but don't have good mechanisms in place for listening, then team members grow frustrated and impatient. All failures of listening are, at root, failures of patience. Building clear channels of communication that allow team members to be heard, challenge the status quo, express fears, voice options, spur debate, admit mistakes, and ultimately drive to agreement is a vital part of becoming a Patient Organization.

I will spend time in Part III challenging you about the strategies and tactics your Organizational Operating System relies on to create productive meetings because 1) they are such an important organizational channel of communication, and 2) they are often poorly structured, terribly run, and painful to sit through.

Many organizations never establish a solid rhythm for their meeting structure. Meetings are ad hoc, vague, or drifting. Team members want to know that, *Okay, now is the time when we talk about X. This is the time to plan strategy for Y, or give feedback on Z.* This builds their feelings of certainty and relatedness because they know what's coming, who will be involved, how their time will be invested, and how it aligns with the larger purpose.

For millions of years, the seasons ruled our lives, and that rhythm remains ingrained in us. Perhaps growing up involved in a family farm has made me especially aware of the pattern, but as someone who has run four very seasonal companies and coached leadership teams at hundreds of others, I can tell you that there is something magical about the ninety-day mark I keep returning to. Whether I bring this up at a nonprofit or a major corporation, leaders tend to agree when I point it out, that things need a kind of reset every three months. I think this is due to the natural changing of the seasons.

As I'll cover in Part III, I believe a strong OOS insures that every individual at an organization will be communicated with, heard, confirmed, and aligned at least every ninety days, or once a season. Similarly, I will ask if your OOS is guiding a meeting inventory to test the utility, labeling, attendance, etc., of every single meeting at the organization every ninety days. You know, out with the old, in with the new, just as you do every season with the clothes in your closet (or in my case, the back of my car).

Here, I want to point out that many of the roadblocks to getting to and maintaining *yes* on the question of being *heard* stem from language. As I said early in Part II, *it's all semantics.* Language matters. Too many leaders carefully plan a meeting but don't have the patience to name it with care and accuracy. What you call the meeting communicates among other things the type of communication channel it will provide for team members and how they can expect to listen and to be heard in it.

This is the same principle I argued for in our discussions of core values and an organization's *why*. You can't enjoy *yes* without getting the language right. Whether you're naming core values or a weekly meeting, lazy, loose, or conflicting language means people don't believe the same thing, and as I've pointed out, your organization is nothing more than the belief of its members. Getting the language wrong isn't a mere oversight, but an existential threat, and leaders can't build a Patient Organization without understanding this. Refusal to be patient and have the guts to name a meeting is a clear sign of dysfunction and confusion, and a weak leader.

As leaders build patience and make progress toward *yes* on the Seven Questions, they create context for all communication. Making team members feel that they are heard is not as simple as ten minutes to bend a supervisor's ear each week. If they are getting to and maintaining *yes* on belonging, believing, accountability, and measurement, then team members will share with leaders a common language and a sense of the big picture. *Why are we having this conversation?* Those who belong and believe understand how their feedback fits into the organization's purpose and strengthens core values alignment.

This larger context helps not only meetings, but mentoring and general reporting too. Like meetings, those communication channels are too often one-way and top-down. I'll discuss strategies for effective reporting and mentoring in Part III, but working toward *yes* on the other questions encourages team members to see everything in those kinds of conversations in terms of the organization's overarching purpose and core values.

Prioritizing listening isn't some touchy-feely, patronizing exercise. Done correctly, it's a vital way for the Patient Organization to leverage strengths and overcome weaknesses, to exploit opportunities, and avoid threats. Picture a topo map or navigational chart where hazards, channels, markers, weather forecasts, etc., are all out in the open.

Understanding and embracing the way that team members are heard builds deep reservoirs of trust in them—the foundation of a model I called EATT in Part I. It's the prerequisite for any organization to be a living, growing thing, as opposed to a soulless machine. Team members who are heard in positive ways have enough trust to voice dissent, take risks, and admit mistakes, to evolve and adapt. They are free to engage in the fearless System 2 thinking that drives competitive advantage.

AM I HEARD?

Follow the prompts below, then at the end, after you have answered all of the prompts, rate how close your organization is to attaining and maintaining *yes* on this question by circling one:

FAR AWAY   MANY MILES   RIGHT AROUND THE CORNER   THERE

Grab a piece of paper and follow these prompts:

PROMPTS

1. What percentage of your time is spent listening to team members?

2. On a scale of 1–10, how would attendees rate meeting effectiveness on average at your organization?

3. When is the last time you took a meeting inventory, assessing the utility, name, attendance, etc. of every meeting at the organization?

Review your answers using my highly unscientific key, on the next page—and don't fudge. Remember, you're the one with the answers, and you probably know in your gut, without reading another word, how far you are from *yes*.

KEY

1. If your initial answer to Prompt 1 is less than 10 percent, you're **FAR AWAY** from *yes*; less than 20 percent, you're **MANY MILES** away. If it's 30 percent or more, you're **RIGHT AROUND THE CORNER** or **THERE**.

2. If you can't initially answer Prompt 2 because you don't ask attendees to rate meetings, you're **FAR AWAY**. If the answer was lower than 7, you're **FAR AWAY**. If you can honestly answer 7 or above, you're **RIGHT AROUND THE CORNER** or **THERE**.

3. If your initial answer to Prompt 3 is more than ninety days, you're somewhere between **MANY MILES** and **FAR AWAY**.

Am I Being Developed?

Yes means...

Organization: *We have a system that helps team members take charge of their development.*

Team member: *I understand, embrace, and control how I am developed.*

DEVELOPMENT OF TEAM members is critical not just when it comes to sharpening skills and building competitive advantages, but it is yet another place where the Seven Questions allow you to combat the depressingly low engagement numbers I have quoted from Gallup. True development allows team members to tune into WIIFM—What's In It for Me—and to connect their personal *why* to the organization's *why*.

Team members who understand and appreciate opportunities for development have greater motivation, trust, and loyalty. Attaining and maintaining *yes* to this question keeps them belonging and believing, although as I'll discuss later, the relationship is circular: *maintaining* yes *on the previous five questions should also provide an organic path to* yes *on this one.*

Leaders often underestimate the power of *development* because they take a narrow, impatient view of it. I say "development," and they think training, certifications, a safety course, a conference, continuing education, etc. All of those are fine and have their place, but *yes* to this question requires a broader more patient perspective of development.

The things I just mentioned tend to come from on high. They are predicated on a one-way, top-down approach to development. True development is both more complex and simpler than that.

Development is more complex in the context of the Seven Questions because it's one of the main planks in building a Patient Organization and not just a box to check: *yes, Joe had his safety training . . . Sue took that online spreadsheets course . . .* Sure, those things are part of the equation, but development should be seen in relief against the rest of the Seven Questions—belonging, believing, accountability, metrics, and, especially, being heard. How does this team member's growth align with the organization's growth? How does his or her development align with the organization's core values and its *why*? How can individual needs be met and skills boosted in ways that allows a team member to get to *yes* on belonging?

Of course, development can include a Microsoft certification or equipment training, but it might also mean a weekly conversation with a leader. It could mean work on changing a particular habit, eliminating a regular duty to make time for thinking, or a teaching assignment. Strategic shuffling, rotations, cross-training of the positions that are part of a given job in ways that make sense for both the organization and the individual can fall under the development umbrella too.

> A PATH FOR DEVELOPMENT SHOULD EMERGE ORGANICALLY.

That's the complicated part.

In a way, though, the process I'm describing is simpler than the usual top-down view, too, because as I'll discuss in Part III, if your OOS is ensuring that you are maintaining a *yes* answer to the previous five questions, *a path for development should emerge organically.* If the team member can say, yes, I believe in the core values and the *why* that the organization has clearly presented, I understand my positions, what I am accountable for, and how my work is measured, then he or she should be able to say, I need to work on X and Y. Here are the skills I must learn or sharpen to contribute to WIIFM and my organization.

The Seven Questions are tightly interwoven, and in a very real sense, team members begin working on Question 6, *Am I developed?* the day that they and the organization start working on Question 1, *Do I belong?* Part of belonging, remember, is being able to say *yes,* I have or can develop the skillsets needed for my positions.

This more organic and holistic view of development puts the team member in charge. I'll discuss this more in Part III, but development can't be done *to* or *for* someone. The organization should be *with* team members as they embrace their own development.

My coach, Greg Walker, and I use the phrase "two lives working on one" rather than "mentoring" precisely because I don't like the top-down relationship this development term implies. This kind of mutually beneficial relationship and the broader view of development I'm advocating require patience. It's much easier to think about a standard training regimen, but helping team members take control of their own development sews patience into the fabric of the organization too. It builds trust and loyalty and encourages them to take the long view of a personal *why* that's intertwined with the organizational *why.* Just as leaders must have the patience to work *on* a business, they must also have the patience to allow individuals who want to progress to work *on* themselves.

All of this might sound like it requires large amounts of additional work. The journey requires patience, as I said, but in the aggregate, it actually takes less work. As team members progress on their own development, they create templates for their positions and for individuals throughout the organization. *Yes* to this and the other questions over time provides useful, organic, employee-created collaterals, including process, procedure, maintenance, training, and development materials that can be used in the future, saving leaders and the Patient Organization tons of time. A good OOS helps you repeat and capture this effort, as I'll explain in Part III.

AM I BEING DEVELOPED?

Follow the prompts below, then at the end, after you have answered all of the prompts, rate how close your organization is to attaining and maintaining *yes* on this question by circling one:

FAR AWAY   MANY MILES   RIGHT AROUND THE CORNER   THERE

Grab a piece of paper and follow these prompts:

PROMPTS

1. What's the first word that comes to mind when someone says "development?"

2. Who is in charge of team members' development at your organization?

3. How often do leaders meet with team members to discuss their development?

Review your answers using my highly unscientific key, on the next page—and don't fudge. Remember, you're the one with the answers, and you probably know in your gut, without reading another word, how far you are from *yes*.

KEY

1. If you initially answered "training," to Prompt 1 you're probably **FAR AWAY**.

2. If your initial answer to Prompt 2 was anything other than "team members," you're probably **FAR AWAY**.

3. If you initially answered more than ninety days to Prompt 3, you're somewhere between **FAR AWAY** and **RIGHT AROUND THE CORNER**. If you said ninety days or less, you could be **THERE** or close to it.

Do I Have Balance?

Yes means...

> **Organization:** *We are honest about our work loads and have in place mechanisms that allow for balancing.*

> **Team member:** *I understand and embrace my organization's work–life balance mechanisms and actively participate in our goal of balance, I am balanced.*

"ALL WORK AND no play makes Jack a dull boy."

Okay, Jack Nicholson's character in *The Shining* did not turn out to be the best employee—repetitive documents, murder, neglect of facilities—but he got that old aphorism just right. The team member who never takes time to recharge can begin to produce work that's as dull and meaningless as the sentence Jack typed over and over for hundreds of pages in that creepy old hotel.

I saw this phenomenon when I ran my own companies, in both team members and myself, their fearless captain. When I left accounting to strike out on my own, I was deeply into bicycle racing, and one of my critical success factors was to train on my bike one hundred and fifty days a year, so I could maintain my racing weight of 178 pounds. I did my best to make it, but when work got the better of me and I was sitting at my desk in mid-afternoon, my team would say, "Hey, Walt, have you ridden your bike yet today? Get out of here. You're making us nervous."

They knew that I would return refreshed and full of creative energy—and nearly always in a stellar mood. A bike ride was the break I needed for maximum creativity, but I'd had to skip it during the crazy audit seasons that dominate accounting. I had not yet fleshed out the Seven Questions. Still, I knew on some level that I was not a *yes* in answering the question, *Do I belong?* at my accounting job, so I self-selected out. I built a company where I could answer *yes*, and I tried to make sure that my team members could find balance, too. If they needed a mental break to hit the gym, meditate, or whatever, that was fine with me as long as they cleared it with the team and didn't drop the ball on anything. A fun example is we knew Chief—one of my Harvard grads—was a ten o'clock person, just one of those humans that was not awake before nine o'clock. The team knew it, she knew it, the organization knew it, and she belonged.

Balance exists in two realms for each of your people, workload and lifeload. Knowing where team members are in balance by taking a constant inventory is a key driver for patience. The two intersect in all sorts of ways. For instance, summers were busy at Layline, and the hours could be long, but our purpose and core values revolved around sailing, so it was understood that people would take off days, sometimes even a full week, to go to a regatta or participate on a sailboat racing team. We made sure that everyone knew when they were taking off and that they were backfilled and covering for each other. The system was fair, honest, and clearly conveyed. Some balance issues stem from personality, or even nature, you might say. Chief absolutely brought it when she was awake. It took some time as a team to understand that this would not happen before ten o'clock in the morning. As a team, we decided that she would start and leave later, so that we could enjoy her at her fullest.

Chief was balanced, work was balanced, and SCARF needs were met. In all such instances, team members knew what was coming and who was covering for whom, so their sense of certainty, relatedness, and fairness was intact. The arrangement relied on autonomy, since people still had to take charge of their schedules and complete their projects, and those who pulled their weight tended to have a healthy status within the tribe. Like me after my bike rides, they also returned with heads clear and creative juices flowing. Their productivity was usually higher and recharged, and with SCARF needs met, they could engage in System 2 thinking.

Patience depends on the longevity and stamina of the team, and organizations that don't address balance head-on will never become Patient Organizations. They tend to fall down here in the same ways they do on the rest of the 7Qs. The failures most often involve poor communication and a lack of empowerment.

First of all, balance is not only different for everyone, but it's also different for individual team members, depending on the week, month, or year. There's the obvious stuff—a new baby, a sick parent, an illness—and lots that's less obvious—burnout, beloved hobbies, new domestic duties. A top-down, singular approach will achieve resentment, not balance, and it will SCARF people to no end. As with development, team members need to be empowered to take charge of their own balance, and that's only possible with good communication and a lack of fear.

As I'll discuss in Part III, maintaining *yes* to balance requires clarity, honesty, and regular communication, all functions of your OOS. Questions about balance must be addressed at least—you guessed it—once a season, every ninety days at minimum. What's going on with team members outside of the organization? What's their outlook for the next ninety days, and what are leaders anticipating?

In what has become a famous story, Facebook COO Sheryl Sandberg, also author of *Lean In: Women, Work and the Will to Lead*, asked some of the most powerful executives in the world at the World Economic Forum in Davos, Switzerland, how many had ever initiated a discussion about possible childbearing down the road with female employees. Not a single hand went up. Sheryl wasn't surprised. HR departments tell you the topic is taboo, but her point was that such open discussions with valued team members could actually help both women and the organizations they're part of to plan better.

Of course, we should respect privacy, but we have become too insistent that any and all personal information is off the table. As I'll argue in Part III, on how to maintain *yes*, it's often helpful to both the team member and the organization to have a conversation about what's going on in life that might affect work, and I will ask if your OOS is facilitating this. My go-to metaphor here is the sea mammal that returns to the depths refreshed, swimming and hunting better after it's had sufficient time to recharge, breathing O2 on the surface. Team members need to be honest about how and why they want to recharge, take a break, get some space to think, breathe.

Organizations must be honest, too, and having policies and rules in place is no guarantee. Too many companies aren't clear about core values that mean working long hours as a deadline nears or a season gets in full swing. False advertising around balance expectations is one of the ways organizations wind up with team members who don't belong and who then spread dysfunction.

The last of the Seven Questions about balance cycles back directly to the first, on belonging. I did not belong at the firm when I became a CPA and took my first job, partly because I could never align to the firm's *yes* regarding the subject of balance. The team members at the company I started, who were passionate about sailing and did belong, found a balance that for many was ideal.

Getting the balance right for myself and my team took patience. Figuring out workarounds because of illness, childbirth, or even simple mental breaks requires patience. But *yes* to balance returns that patience in spades. It allows both team members and the organization to plan intelligently, think long-term, build stamina, and operate consistently at full bore. As I have said, with patience comes consistency, with consistency comes stamina, and with stamina comes great repeatable results.

DO I HAVE BALANCE?

Follow the prompts below, then at the end, after you have answered all of the prompts, rate how close your organization is to attaining and maintaining *yes* on this question by circling one:

FAR AWAY   MANY MILES   RIGHT AROUND THE CORNER   THERE

Grab a piece of paper and follow these prompts:

PROMPTS

1. Find three random members of the team—one senior leader, one mid-level person, and someone on the frontline—and ask, *on a scale of one to ten, how well are you able to balance work and life these days?*

2. Ask the same three team members to rate on a scale of one to ten how well the organization understands and tries to help balance their life needs with work.

3. When is the last time you had a conversation with a team member about life outside of the organization and his or her needs in balancing it with work?

Review your answers using my highly unscientific key, on the next page—and don't fudge. Remember, you're the one with the answers, and you probably know in your gut, without reading another word, how far you are from *yes*.

KEY

1. For Prompt 1, if the three random members initially answered from seven to ten, you might be **RIGHT AROUND THE CORNER** or even **THERE**. Less than seven means you're somewhere between **FAR AWAY** and **MANY MILES**.

2. For Prompt 2, if they initially answered from seven to ten, you're might be **RIGHT AROUND THE CORNER** or even **THERE**. Less than seven means you're somewhere between **FAR AWAY** and **MANY MILES**.

3. If you initially answered more than ninety days for Prompt 3, you're **FAR AWAY**. If you said ninety days or less, you might be **RIGHT AROUND THE CORNER** or even **THERE**.

PART III

ATTAINING AND MAINTAINING *YES*

CHAPTER 6

AN ORGANIZATIONAL OPERATING SYSTEM DRIVES BUSINESS

MY FAVORITE METAPHOR for an Organizational Operating System (OOS) is the waterwheel. Powering human endeavors for millennia, from quaint mill pond wheels that grind flour and saw logs to industries harvesting the flow and drop of the Erie and Augusta Canals. As a matter of fact, the turbines at the base of Hoover Dam are, in essence, waterwheels. Waterwheels are powerful, steady, patient, and versatile. They require tending and maintenance, but they essentially run on their own, with great torque and momentum, powered by an endless renewable source.

Like a waterwheel, a good OOS powers your organization. It captures the source of an organization's energy and direction, and with a little maintenance, it, too, runs on its own. The Seven Questions and the tools of your OOS are the buckets on that wheel, the fins on the turbine. If you can keep filling those buckets by aligning everyone to *yes* on the Seven Questions and maintaining an effective OOS, then you can harness incredible energy.

As I explained in Part I, an OOS provides an efficient, repeatable way for businesses to clarify exactly who is responsible for what, and to prioritize and focus the company's limited resources against its vision (why it exists, what it does, where it is going). An OOS has a concrete set of tools that help owners set priorities, review team members, track numbers, and, most of all, communicate. They often include other tools that help leaders develop marketing strategies, and set aside time to plan following a detailed timeline and agenda.

Every organization has some sort of OOS, whether the leaders know it or not. When I ran Layline, I had various systems, procedures, and tools that together formed an organic operating system. It did the job and mirrored elements of today's popular systems, but a lack of understanding of my own methods was a drawback. For example, not knowing that my core values were core values made it hard to give them teeth.

One advantage of the prepackaged Organizational Operating Systems available today is that they come with a complete set of clearly articulated tools. There's less guesswork and there are fewer gaps—or at least, that should be the case. An effective OOS should ensure that you consistently communicate, maintain and refine how folks answer *yes* to the Seven Questions. If it does not, it might have terrific features, but the gaps will hurt the organization. Doing the hard work, what I call the *Heavy Lift*, of defining the "first yes" is not always baked into an OOS, but, once defined, the OOS will maintain them and help keep them strong. Choosing the right OOS depends on the needs and personality of your organization.

I work with the Entrepreneurial Operating System (EOS®), which I think is extremely effective at maintaining seven *yeses*. Other OOSs include 4DX, Gazelles/Rockefeller Habits/Scaling Up, The Advantage, and Holacracy. Some call Google's OKR (Objectives and Key Results) an OOS, but I think it is just *one piece* of a good OOS. All of them have some excellent features. I hope that by understanding what I have written, you will be able to build your own rubric that maps and measures the effectiveness and fit of your OOS.

You might determine that the system you have developed organically already does this work. If that's the case, I hope that Part III, on answering *yes* to the Seven Questions, will help you keep the buckets on your waterwheel full. There is a reason, however, that you picked up this book and are still reading. Whatever the gaps between the initial dream you had for your organization and the way it has actually grown, your OOS probably plays a role. I hope you'll learn more about Organizational Operating Systems with an open mind and consider how they might help you.

The purpose of an OOS is to enable you to consistently *lead* your team through the Seven Questions. It is that simple.

An effective OOS builds patience and offers an incredible competitive advantage, but installing one is not easy. In my experience, it takes eighteen months before the system begins to yield the kind of patience I'm encouraging, and full implementation takes about three years. Someone at the organization must own the OOS and oversee this effort, since owners typically can't devote the necessary time.

And, of course, there will be resistance.

Every problem at an organization, at root, is a people problem, and even engaged people resist change. The resistance put up by those who aren't engaged, who don't belong or believe in your core values or purpose, will be even greater. This is another reason that the 7Qs are vital, whether or not you decide to install a new OOS. Asking everyone in the organization to get aligned with *yes* on believing, belonging, accountability, measurement, hearing, development, and balance fills the buckets of whatever system is powering the organization. Eliminating those who can't or won't align with *yes* empowers those who are engaged, and builds patience for all.

In this section, I'll share some exercises for doing the "Heavy Lift" to lay the corner stones that make up "First Yeses," and I will point out/mark where your OOS plays a role in maintaining *yes* with a check mark: ✓. The work of determining the First Yeses begins with the organization. It does the heavy lifting on Questions 1–3 because this attacks the big structural issues—core values, why, how, what, positions. Question 4 (measurement) is the pivot, with the organization doing half the work and the individual the other half. The team member takes the lead on the last three—hearing, development, and balance.

OOS CHECKLIST

In this section, I'll share some exercises for doing the "Heavy Lift" to lay the corner stones that make up "First Yeses," and I will point out/mark where your OOS plays a role in maintaining yes with a check mark.

I spend the most time on the questions that demand the most work of the organization (primarily Sr. Leadership). Because the organization shoulders 80 percent of the burden on Question 1—*Do I belong?*—I give it by far the most space. By the time we get to Question 7, on balance, the individual is doing 80 percent of the work, and my advice on getting started can be much briefer. This does not mean that attaining and maintaining *yes* on the last three questions is unimportant. It's actually vital, but if you are at *yes* on the first four, then you have significant momentum, and team members who belong and believe, and are accountable begin to take charge of their measures, how they are heard, developed, and balanced.

Once you determine *yes* on all 7Qs, the practical tools of your OOS keep you there, turning a powerful, patient waterwheel that provides its own momentum and the kind of competitive advantage that leaves the competition floundering in the outflow below your dam.

CHAPTER 7

PRACTICAL STEPS TO THE FOUNDATIONAL SEVEN *YESES*

LIKE OBI-WAN KENOBI'S mantra—*Use the Force*—hovering in Luke Skywalker's head, my father's words of wisdom have echoed in my ears for decades. Unlike young Skywalker, however, I did not turn off my targeting computer in response. I suppose I turned it on, and Father's aphorism became the foundation for my understanding of how organizations work and for the Seven Questions. In organizational terms, the *force* is people, the water (powering the OOS waterwheel), and, just as in the *Star Wars* movies, those who learn to use it wisely unleash incredible power.

Leadership, with the help of everyone, must do the Heavy Lifting of defining all *positions* (a task more difficult and useful than that of defining *jobs*) to determine who belongs where, which tasks are falling through the cracks, and what duplication can be eliminated. Once the organization has defined all positions and installed workable architecture, it can decide, along with team members, if they have or can develop the skills necessary to truly belong in the positions they occupy.

In this section, I will share practical strategies for the Heavy Lift—finding and refining your core values—the first step to attaining and maintaining *yes*. I'll show a tool from an active OOS that you can use to communicate them to team members and to rate everyone's degree of alignment with those values on the road to *yes*. In the section on accountability, we will explore a practical approach to defining positions within an organization that I learned during my sailing days from a consulting organizational psychologist who worked with our race team.

The following sections will explore steps to attaining and maintaining yes on the 7Qs. The graph below shows how much effort an organization should put into this step (arrow on the left) and how much effort the individual should put in (arrow on the right).

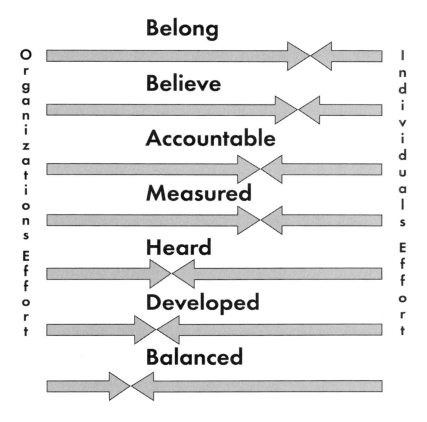

The arrows relate to the 7Qs by showing the percentage of work the organization puts in (arrow on the left) and the percentage of work the individual puts in (arrow on the right) to attain and maintain yes to the question.

Attaining and Maintaining *Yes* on Belonging

Work on *yes*

Organization: 80%
Individual: 20%

Organization 80%	Individual 20%

THIS IS WHY the question *Do I belong?* ranks first on our list and demands the most work from the organization. It is foundational. Surrounding yourself with people who can enthusiastically say, *yes I belong*, as I have argued, eliminates untold problems and builds patience like nothing else. It is not half the battle; in a very real sense, it *is* the battle.

My estimate is that about 80 percent of determining *yes* on this question falls on the organization, and around 20 percent on the individual. The organization's leadership must think deeply about, discover, and develop its core values to pave the way for maintaining *yes*. It must articulate them clearly and integrate them into every level of the organization—and, as author Patrick Lencioni says, *give them teeth*. Faced with core values that permeate every strategy, project, and decision, the individual then must decide if his or her core values align with those of the organization.

Defining Core Values

Discovering, or uncovering, your organization's core values and communicating them consistently and clearly is half the work of *yes* on the question *Do I belong?* I began this book talking about the dream that is the seed from which every organization grows. Core values are the manifestation of and prerequisite for that dream. The owner who pictured her business long before she started it saw herself surrounded by people who shared certain values, people she liked, people who belonged. In terms of the waterwheel I described earlier, core values are the axle at the very center (yep, the *core*). They are the thing that makes the waterwheel work, the backbone of momentum, the point where everything—including patience—comes together. They guide long-term strategy as well as small quick decisions, and they are one of two key criteria in deciding who belongs.

What do I mean by core values? The phrase has become popular in business circles, but even many of those promoting the idea seem unsure of its meaning. I define *core values* as the philosophy or attitude that shapes how team members treat each other, clients, and other stakeholders. Core values are the deeply held principles that set the organization apart, give it its unique personality and a competitive edge. They are the cultural foundation beneath every meeting, memo, and watercooler conversation.

At Layline, our core values could be summarized as PC3: be positive, cheerful, cognizant, challenge your work, and try to ask three questions before you respond. These were the key elements of a mindset that I wanted to inform every decision and color every interaction—whether with a coworker, a customer, a vendor, or me. A large software and client-service company I have worked with describes its core values as: passionate, disciplined, client-focused, dependable, and engaged. Another client, a grocery store chain, lists its core values as: take ownership, treat customers like family, work well with teammates, and be willing to learn and improve.

The organizations above have strikingly different core values. But each set reflects the personality of the organization, its vision, and the attitude of team members. Being *client-focused* and *dependable* has a different nuance than *treating customers like family*. Neither approach is better than the other. Each reflects a unique mindset at the heart of how a particular organization does business. A team member who excels at being client-focused and dependable might recoil at the idea of treating customers like family, or always asking three questions before answering one. Such a person might align with the core values of the software company in my example, but struggle for years without ever aligning to *yes* at Layline or the grocery chain.

I'm providing examples here to illustrate what true core values are and how they work on a practical level. When I do this in conversations with leaders and business owners, they frequently realize that the things posted on the company website, hung above the reception desk, or printed in the training manual do not represent the organization's true core values.

I have also found that it's helpful and sometimes even more illuminating to consider what core values are *not*.

A core value is not a goal. Endless companies now list some version of "a sustainable future" as a core value. Sorry, that's a goal, not a value. It does not describe the way team members interact with each other and customers on a daily basis. Patrick Lencioni, author of *The Five Dysfunctions of a Team* and many other books and articles on the subject, has shaped my thinking on core values. He makes the point that an aspiration is not a core value and recounts the story of a Fortune 500 CEO telling him without hesitation that "a sense of urgency" is a core value at his organization because *no one has it yet.*[14] Aspirations are important—*we need to become more X or have more Y*—but should not be confused with core values. Core values represent today's deeply held attitude, not tomorrow's target.

A core value is not an obvious baseline. Qualities such as honesty, integrity, and trustworthiness sound like core values, but short of organized crime syndicates, every team member at every organization should have these qualities, right? Lencioni calls such attributes "permission to play" values. They represent a minimum behavioral standard throughout society and don't distinguish an organization in any way. They are not core values.

A core value is not marketing. Once upon a time, a large company I heard of trademarked the phrase "culture of caring" and insisted in its marketing that in addition to being "warm, welcoming, and humble," its team members would be empathetic enough to make a difference in people's lives. In 2016, news emerged that thousands of the employees were opening fraudulent accounts customers hadn't authorized, to collect bonuses. The warm fuzzy lines on the website suddenly looked like empty slogans. Core values are internal and sacrosanct, as Lencioni says. They are the secret sauce that creates patience and momentum for a company. If it makes sense to use them in some marketing materials, fine, but first and foremost, they must be the internal engine running the organization. Hollow announcements of generic core values have a way of coming back to bite you on the rear end.

A core value is not a skill or an IQ. Most business owners want smart employees, but most also know that intelligence doesn't

---

14   Patrick M. Lencioni, "Make Your Values Mean Something,"
Harvard Business Review, July 2002, https://hbr.org/2002/07/
make-your-values-mean-something

automatically mean team player. If I hired a genius at Layline who thought he had all the answers and didn't need to ask questions, he wouldn't last long. If a medical practice establishes *personal warmth* and a *friendly bedside manner* as a core value, plenty of skilled but socially awkward surgeons won't belong there.

A core value is not cookie-cutter or industry specific. Core values come from deep soul searching about what's important to and special about an organization. When they're real, they attract and inspire people who belong. When platitudes are fired off instead, they create cynicism, not inspiration, and thereby attract people who simply need jobs. One client of mine frames the company's core values this way: "We believe in the power of listening, hearing and taking action." There's no way for you to guess that this is a janitorial supply firm, but seeing the way the organization integrates those deeply held values into its operation, I can tell you, is inspiring. This is what's important to the company's leaders and separates it from the competition.

A core value is not accidental. As the center of the dream that becomes a business, core values often gestate for years within the business owner before they guide his or her company. Over time, additional values often gestate within the organization—Lencioni calls them "accidental values." They might be positive or negative, but they are unintentional. They should be watched closely and not confused with core values.

DISCOVER YOUR CORE VALUES

Here's another thing that a core value is not—a political candidate. Which is to say, the process of deciding on your core values is not a democratic one. It falls on the leadership team and owner—not on all employees. Remember the start of this section, where I said that around 80 percent of determining *yes* to the question *Do I belong?* falls on the organization. Owners had certain principles in mind when they began turning their dream into the reality of a business. There are particular attitudes that they would like to hear in the hallways, see conveyed in reports, and have transmitted to clients. Passing the responsibility for articulating those core values to employees is disingenuous and likely to result in chaos.

How should core values be articulated? By way of background, I highly recommend Patrick Lencioni's Harvard Business Review article I mentioned earlier: "Make Your Values Mean Something." Then, use his core values articulation exercise—a three-step process outlined in his book The Advantage.

Test your results against our earlier discussion of core values. Make sure your list doesn't include distant goals or aspirations, skills, or what Lencioni calls "permission-to-play" values (honesty, integrity, etc.). Most of all, make sure that the values you end up with are sincere and unique to your organization. Authentic, clearly articulated core values will fire up the troops, building cohesion and patience. Hollow "values" that smack of a marketing campaign can result in eye-rolls and even disengagement.

Like the end of a good novel, the core values that emerge from this exercise might seem both surprising and inevitable. *We've always emphasized that we want people to enjoy their jobs, so it makes sense that "fun at work"* is on the board, but we never articulated the fact that this is one of the four core values this place runs on. Some of your core values might be a little edgy if that's who you are as an organization. One of my clients lists *no jerks* (they use a more graphic word, but I'll keep it clean here) as a core value. This is something the organization feels passionately about, and it expresses the attitude in passionate terms. That's fine. Core values are for internal use. If authenticity demands colorful language, quirky phrasing, humor, or a dash of vitriol, go for it.

HEAVY LIFT—EXERCISING PATIENCE

GIVE YOUR CORE VALUES TEETH

You've established your core values. Now what? At many organizations, core values are a one-time exercise. They're named hastily, printed on a plaque somewhere or mentioned at a retreat, and begin to rot. That's unfortunate but understandable. Truly integrating your core values into the organization, making them the touchstone for who belongs and how decisions get made is painful. The process requires deep reserves of patience. It puts new pressure on leaders and holds them and team members to higher standards. Some, you will quickly see, cannot find *yes* on belonging. They will have to be let go, or, as often happens, will realize themselves that they can't realize *yes* and self-select out.

If you take core values seriously, though, and use them to underpin *yes* on belonging and the rest of the 7Qs, you unleash a force that would impress even Obi-Wan Kenobi. They become a key factor in *leading* rather than merely *managing*, as I discussed earlier. Since virtually all problems at an organization are people problems, using core values alignment for *yes* on belonging eliminates endless problems before they are born. Imagine the power of an organization where everyone belongs and is aligned with the core values. Imagine the patience that gets built by having this consistent lens through which all strategy and decisions are viewed.

The first step is to begin assessing everyone's alignment with the core values to gauge whether or not they can say *yes, I belong.*✓ Begin with the leaders in the room, the ones who decided on the core values in the first place. How you do this is up to you. The Entrepreneurial Operating System (EOS®) uses something called the People Analyzer. The basic method is to write the core values across the top of the board and list names down the side. Starting with your leadership team, ask everyone in the room, "Okay, how does Bob rate on our core value of Gives A S**t" (GAS)? The EOS® rating scale is Plus (Bob's very GAS), Plus-Minus (Bob has some work to do in this area), or Minus (Bob is failing in GAS). This gives some degree of objectivity to a fairly subjective measure.

The exercise leader should tally the ratings from Bob's fellow leaders and post them on the board under each core value. After Bob, move on to Susan, then Lisa, then Dave until the whole room has been rated. Is this an uncomfortable exercise? You bet it is, and it, or something similar, should be done for everyone in the organization. People, at least some of them, will begin to feel SCARFed—that is, they'll feel a threat to their status, certainty, autonomy, relatedness, and fairness.

With a rubric like Wickman's People Analyzer as a consistently used and known OOS tool, team members will begin to seriously assess whether they belong at the organization.✓ They will ask themselves—and continually be asked by leaders—if their values align with the organization's core values. I will talk more about rubrics later, but this tool for establishing expectations and metrics, especially subjective measures, is a vital part of US education today and familiar to anyone under age forty. Communicating the organization's core values through a specific tool like the People Analyzer provides team members with a fundamental rubric. They are now aware of the deepest expectations at the organization. *Well, it's been made abundantly clear to me that I should be positive, cheerful, and cognizant. I should challenge my work, and ask three questions first. I'm a smart and hard worker, but no one would describe me as positive or cheerful. Lots of offices don't value those qualities, so maybe I'm at the wrong one.*

If you have not attempted to implement core values until now, understand that the effort won't be realized overnight. This book is called *The Patient Organization* for a reason. In my experience, it takes six to eight months of hard work for the initiative to take root. During that time, your core values should become a part of all hiring, planning, and strategizing. They should be present in meetings and memos, the backbone of collaborative efforts. Leaders should demonstrate clearly that core values aren't slogans but a decision matrix.✓ *If we choose X or decide Y, how does that align with our core values?*

Team members will begin to use core values to make their own decisions, too; at least, those who belong will. Those who can't reach this degree of alignment need to go.✓ Remember, patience does not mean putting up with jerks.

Those who belong and are aligned to your core values will feel more engaged, even inspired, by your ubiquitous core values. Make them a part of all training and training materials, all conversations, onboarding, measurements (more on this later), etc. Use them to recruit, hire, and fire.✓

The Interview Promise

Unfortunately, one can't really interview for core values. Ask a dozen job candidates if they are positive, cheerful, and cognizant, and you'll get a dozen *yeses*. Few will answer, *No, I'm actually fairly dour and unaware.* Instead, I recommend putting your core values out there so strongly during all interviews that they become a promise to new hires: *John, I am making a promise to you, the same one I make to everyone who works here. I am going to surround you with people who have these core values, so let me explain them for you. They are x, y, z. Now, if you have these values, our organization will be heaven for you, nirvana. If not, it will be hell on earth. You'll be miserable, everyone around you will be miserable, and before long, either the organization or I will flush you out. Does this sound like a fair promise?* This approach will be part of your OOS.✓

Once someone is hired, they must be continually asked to reaffirm that they belong. *You did an excellent job on project X, which demonstrates this core value, however, you're slipping in this other area, which shows a lack of alignment with our core value of x. Which value do you think you are struggling with? Which one is your strongest?* You get the idea and it is part of your OOS to put into place this type of work.✓

Like Patrick Lencioni says, you're giving your core values teeth.

EOS® offers advice and systemizes this as part of their suggested HR process. If someone is out of alignment with a core value once the implementation is well underway (180 to 270 days in), you must list and clearly communicate at least three examples of this misalignment or you're not likely to be heard. After pointing out the ways that a team member is not meeting the core value standard, give him thirty days to correct course. If he doesn't get it right then, allow another thirty days, but make it clear that continued misalignment at sixty days means that the person does not belong and will be asked to leave. All of this is baked into EOS® as part of your OOS. ✓

DO I HAVE THE NECESSARY SKILLS?
(SEE ACCOUNTABLE.)

Integrating core values and making sure team members are aligned with them gets you only halfway to *yes* on belonging. Employing people with the right skills in the right positions is equally important. At Layline, the most positive, cheerful, cognizant team members would have accomplished little as customer advisors if they didn't have and couldn't develop the basic skills necessary for the seasonal positions attached to that job (vendor relations, buying, html knowledge, etc.).

As I pointed out in Part II, a *job* includes many *positions*, and focusing on them gives you a more thorough inventory than if you only consider mere jobs or titles. In Question 3, *Am I Accountable?* I'll lead you through an exercise that helps you focus on all positions within the organization, rather than on jobs. I'm categorizing that exercise under *accountability*, but it's part of *yes* on belonging too. People need to be clear on which positions they hold as well as the skills needed to fill them before they can get to *yes* on the second-half of belonging: *yes, I have or can develop the skills necessary for my positions.*

Attaining and Maintaining *Yes* on Believing

Work on *yes*

Organization: 80%
Individual: 20%

Organization 80% ▷◁ Individual 20%

YES ON THE question, *Do I Believe?* demands that the organization possess a strong purpose, or *why*, and a clear strategy for achieving it. Team members must then be able to say, *yes I Believe* in that purpose and leadership's strategy for fulfilling it.

Earlier, I cited Gallup stats showing that millennials are five times more likely to be engaged at work when the organization has a strong *why* that they can believe in. This phenomenon doesn't apply only to millennials. We all want lives that have an impact. We all want to work for some larger purpose. As you know well by now, my view of organizations is primarily tribal. Humans are social animals. We survived as a species because we could believe in a common purpose and work together to fulfill it. The need for purpose is embedded in the brains of Homo sapiens, and organizations that ignore it are driving with the brakes on.

Team members who can unhesitatingly say, *yes, I believe* are able to take the long view and rise above the daily minutiae to engage in the System 2 rational thinking discussed earlier. In this way, purpose fosters patience on both an organizational and personal level. Around 80 percent of determining *yes* on the question *Do I Believe?* falls on the organization (Sr. Leadership), which must not only articulate a clear purpose but also an effective strategy (every accountability level) for realizing it. Many organizations solve part of that equation but leave the other half untended.

My thinking about the second of the Seven Questions has been heavily influenced by Simon Sinek, author of *Start with Why.* Most organizations, Sinek argues, start with the *what*—the widgets they produce or services they provide. Some also focus on the *how.* They can communicate how they do what they do, the qualities or processes that set them apart. Very few, however, have given much thought or space to their *why.* Starting with this inner circle—the organization's purpose/why—and working outward to the *what*, in Sinek's view, inspires and builds loyalty like nothing else. He calls these three concentric rings (*why, how, what*) "the Golden Circle" and encourages leaders to start in the center.[15]

Apple is a prime example of a company that starts with *why.* Sinek argues that Apple's *Why* is the belief in challenging the status quo. Apple's, *How,* is we think differently. It's *What* is changing the way people interact with technology. This is no small part of why consumer's line up for city blocks to get the latest Apple gadget the day it is released. Apple's *why* inspires some of the top engineers and

---

15   Simon Sinek, "How great leaders inspire action," filmed September 2009 at TEDxPuget, Newcastle, WY, video, 17:58, https://www.ted.com/talks/ simon_sinek_how_great_leaders_inspire_action

designers in the business, as well as a customer base whose brand loyalty looks a lot like a religion.

The stated purpose of Starbucks is "to inspire and nurture the human spirit—one person, one cup, and one neighborhood at a time." There's no mention of top-quality coffee beans or superior roasting methods. So, breaking this down, the *why* is to inspire and nurture the human spirit; their *how* is one person, one cup, and one neighborhood at a time; and the *what* is comfortable seating, eclectic music, pleasant lighting, Wi-Fi, and friendly baristas. Working outward from the stated purpose, it's easy to see why. Comfortable seating, eclectic music, pleasant lighting, Wi-Fi, and friendly baristas (all part of the *what)* are every bit as important to Starbucks as is quality coffee. The local Starbucks is meant to be a community hub where people work, read, meet, and talk—and drink various beverages in cups. Starbucks's *why,* which is printed on the inside of employees' green aprons so they see it every day, is unique, and guides activity and decision making from the board room to the baristas.

At Layline, our belief was: (Our *why*): Protect our customers' finite weekends/days off. (Our *how*): By carrying the latest and the best, shipping it out fast, and guaranteeing our work 100 percent. We ate it if we missed a delivery date. While I did not know this was a golden circle statement, it was our guide for everything we did. If we were pondering a course, or found ourselves reacting to a situation, we could run it through this filter and come to consistent decisions.

A large industrial rigging client's *why* is: Working Together Safely. *How* is: delivering high-quality, on-schedule, cost-effective work. *What* is: Relationships that last forever. All of their decisions pass through this filter and it is baked into their OOS.

If you can get to a strong *Why* or *Belief* statement, your center, filling in the *How* and *What* are easy. Below are Belief/Why statement examples:

- We believe retail is not dead, as a matter of fact it is very much alive.

- We believe in the power of listening and taking action.

- Partnering with companies to offer the right balance between technology and people.

- Leading people to financial security.

- Delivering repeatable "wow" experiences.

- Through constant never ending improvement of our mind, body, character and spirit, we will enable ourselves and each other to excel.

- We believe in empowering others to accomplish that which they never thought they could.

- Sound is nurturing to one's soul.

- Seniors deserve more.

- Helping with our unique knowledge and capabilities.

- Improving the way people make and use energy.

Replying *yes* on believing begins with the organization's leadership team thinking deeply about its *why* and creating a belief statement that articulates it (I prefer "belief statements" to "mission statements," which are often wordy and too broad in scope. But, you can start with your current mission statement as a guide). My belief statement is: "I believe in freedom." I can expand that this way, "the freedom that comes when owners and leadership teams have the guts to do what it takes to go from good to great, to do what it takes to create a championship organization, when they do this they create freedom for everyone around them, employees, vendors, customers the world at large."

Freedom is my *why*. *How* I achieve it is by being an EOS® Implementer. *What* I create is more time, more money, and less stress for clients. Everything I do is filtered against this belief statement.

A good belief statement is the nut at the center of everything. It should be succinct—just a sentence or two—and clear. It doesn't have to start "We believe," but I recommend beginning with that format as you craft one to keep leaders focused on belief and purpose and not drifting off into the business mission or a distant vision.

Creating a belief statement might seem simple or frivolous, but as you'll see if you make a sincere effort to formulate and integrate one, it is not. Below are some tips on how to get started.

CREATE A BELIEF STATEMENT

Simplify, Focus, Say No. If your Why/How/What statement gives you and your team the ability to Simply, Focus, and Say No, then you have nailed it. Unlike Sinek's outwardly focused, marketing fit message, our belief statement is intended to be an internally used filter first, not as a marketing tool or slogan. Remember, Starbucks doesn't have their belief statement on the door; it is inside the apron, their secret sauce.

Huddle with your leadership team for this exercise, but before you begin, spend some time talking about what a belief statement is and how the organization will use and benefit from it. Have them study Sinek's stuff. Getting buy-in here is crucial. If leaders see this as one of those feel-good exercises with no real-world consequences, then you're wasting your time. Bring up examples of how companies you admire have used their belief statements, whether it is the Apples and Teslas of the world, or smaller organizations you can relate to. In Sinek's Tedx talk, he mentioned we had to find our "why."

Easy format:

We believe (our why):

_____

How we go about living up to our why (or how):

_____

What is ultimately accomplished, in place, done (our what):

_____

Impress upon the leadership team that the statement they help craft will become part of all training, onboarding, meetings, and strategic planning. It will motivate the team, allowing you to focus, simplify, and say no. If they take it seriously, it will make decisions easier and potentially boost the bottom line. It will build patience into the organization by encouraging everyone to check every decision against the big picture. ✓

As with core values, a belief statement that is simply slapped on the website or engraved on a plaque to gather dust is a waste of time. Once you have created the statement, it should be part of your OOS's work to make it effective—to make it become a part of daily conversations. ✓ Include it in all interviews, training, meetings, and onboarding. At the one-on-one seasonal meeting each team member has with a coach, both parties should be assessing how close they are to *yes* on the question *Do I Believe?* If a lack of thinking or doing in the team member's various positions indicates a misalignment with purpose, then leaders should have specific examples that demonstrate ways in which the individual does not seem to be motivated by the organization's *why.* ✓

PLAN TO ACHIEVE YOUR *WHY*

Your OOS should drive your planning and shape your strategy.

Most organizations are no strangers to strategic planning, and each has its preferred methods. After Jim Collins and Jerry Porras published *Built to Last*, their notion of the BHAG (Big Hairy Audacious Goal) became popular as a way to focus long-term ambitions. Other approaches offer different names for that long-term goal and the short-term strategies needed to achieve it. Many find Franklin Covey's notion of scheduling the "big rocks"—your top strategic priories—helpful, rather than sorting through gravel. Google's OKRs (Objectives and Key Results) have gained popularity as a planning tool, as well.

I like the *critical success factor method* to strategic thinking, a method pioneered D. Ronald Daniel of McKinsey and advanced through MITs Jack Rockhart in the 1960s. A vision statement (see your belief statement) is supported by a list of the critical success factors (CSFs) that must manifest in order for the vision to be realized. These are typically the things that need to be in place by the end of the year for the plan to stay on track. Beneath each CSF is a list of one or more goals—targets that help fulfill the vision in smaller steps. Beneath each goal is a list of one or more strategy statements—mini-plans laying out how we accomplish the goals. And, finally, beneath them is a list of the tactics or to-do items that allow us to execute the strategy.

The labels change, but most strategic planning has some version of these elements—the overall vision, the factors critical to its success, and then the goals, strategies, and tactics that you will use to make those factors a reality. I won't suggest which approach you should use here, but in order to maintain *yes* on the question Do I Believe? team members have to agree not only with the purpose—but they must also agree with the organization's priorities and strategies for getting there. Someone who loves the destination but whines for the entire ride because he doesn't like the route is no fun to have in the car, right?

The purpose articulated in the organization's belief statement should be clearly connected to its strategic plan, which should be communicated on a regular basis to team members via your OOS.✔ Seen through the eyes of the individual, it should be apparent how the plan aligns on an organizational level, a team level, and on a WIIFM, individual level.

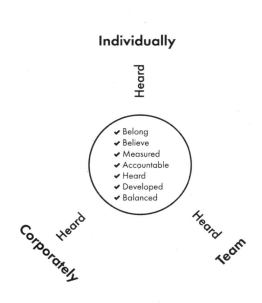

If someone still can't align to your *yes* after the strategy has been fully explained, it's time to invite that budding entrepreneur to go and start his or her own organization.✔

Strategic planning is important, and I love it, but organizations run on people, not plans. The greatest plan in the world is useless if you have not surrounded yourself with people who belong, believe, are accountable, are measured well, and are heard, developed, and balanced. A key impetus for the Seven Questions came from my years of working with leaders on strategic plans and then watching them struggle to execute them. Without a deep well of patience and a way to constantly address those seven key areas, implementation is impossible.

Attaining and Maintaining Yes to Accountability

Work on *yes*

Organization: 65%
Individual: 35%

Organization 65% ▶◀ Individual 35%

ONE OF THE myths that nudged me into writing this book was the notion that millennials lack accountability. In my experience, there was no truth to this stereotype, so I began asking fresh team members what they wanted from work. Across the board, I found that millennials not only want accountability, but also that a lack of clear accountability at their organizations was a major source of frustration.

Too often, the millennials I interviewed said, when talking about job accountabilities, that leaders did not clearly outline or communicate what team members should be thinking about and doing. There was fuzziness about the purpose of their positions and how they connected to larger goals. They weren't always sure about who they reported to for which tasks, or just how far their authority extended.✓ Here yet again, it turned out, millennials wanted what we all want.

And I found that the team members who belonged and believed the most—who had the organization's core values and were behind its *why*—got the most upset about shaky accountability. These were the people who showed up eager to do a good job and, so, they suffered the most frustration when shackled by poor accountability.

Apart from the obvious inefficiencies, this is one of the most damaging aspects of not aligning to *yes* on Question 3—turning the A-players into coal cars. I discussed the neutrally engaged workers I call "coal cars" in Part I—the people who show up and do the required work, who stay off the brakes but add no energy to the organization. We need coal cars, there are plenty out there, 50 percent, but we must be super-diligent not to lose our engaged diamonds to disengagement or neutrality.

Setting up a clear *accountability* structure replaces that frustration with patience. In conjunction with *yes* on the rest of the 7Qs, it allows you to build engagement among top team members and unleashes a powerful force. As I discussed in Part II, maintaining *yes* on this question is a key way of addressing SCARF needs. Clear accountability is absolutely necessary for status, certainty, autonomy, relatedness, and fairness.

Yes on accountability takes serious work—no, your current direct-report or org chart alone won't cut it—but once you've done the work, you save enormous time and energy because you can lead rather than merely manage. People who are clear about their positions, their purpose, and what they need to be thinking and doing every day feel liberated.✓ They have a greater sense of direction. It sounds counterintuitive perhaps, but accountability actually brings freedom. Team members answering *yes* on accountability can work with certainty and autonomy. They know their zone and are comfortable in it.

Yes on accountability improves team cohesion and performance, too. The painstaking work of delineating all positions and making sure that every task, idea, and issue is captured eliminates tensions, insecurities, and petty squabbles. ✓ Team members now know how they relate to everyone else at the organization. They're aware of their own and each other's status, and the fairness quotient rises. Tim, who resented being drafted to help with payroll every Thursday, is no longer annoyed, either because a course correction moves him out of that ad hoc position or because it becomes his, officially.

My example might seem like a distinction without a difference— Tim is doing the exact same work—but *owning* the position, with real accountability, can be the difference between a star and a coal car. People in various positions need to own the processes and procedures that define their work and be partly accountable for developing and refining them. This is why the responsibility of *yes* here begins to shift to the team member, with about 65 percent of the weight shouldered by the organization and the remaining 35 percent by the individual.

Leadership must start the process, though, by pressing an initiative that takes an inventory of everything that needs to be done and every position, setting aside for the moment, jobs and titles.

DEFINE POSITIONS AND SKILLS

My philosophy and the approach I will share with you around creating clear accountability was carved in stone in 2001. During that time, I was a crew member of a sailboat racing program campaigning a Swan 56 for a millionaire out of New York City. Think very high-end, NASCAR-level budgets and a race circuit that went from San Francisco to Newport, Rhode Island, to Antiqua to Sardinia every year. A Swan 56 was crewed by seventeen team members. I was one of them. Our program worked with an organizational psychologist who would gather the team in a room and drill us on our positions.

He would draw a cross-section of a dome-shaped table and then would say: *Gentlemen, hanging off this domed-shaped table are positions that have to capture and sort everything that falls on the table—everything that hits the boat. Imagine a ball bearing drops on this domed table, what's it going to do? It is going to roll. Our goal is to determine our positions so precisely that nothing ever hits the floor or gets lost in confusion. We are going to capture these positions in what we will call a Position Purpose statement. It will go like this: The name of my position is A, the purpose of position A is B, I will fulfill this purpose B by doing C, success will be measured short-term with D and long-term with E. I will report to F, I am part of teams G and H, and I will be coached by I.*

These are the positions I owned on the Swan, each had a full Position Purpose Statement and we kept score of results on scorecards that were reviewed as teams and as individuals with our coach.

My job title as one of seventeen team members was "port jib trimmer," and the positions I held as part of that job are described a little later. I will not go into deep detail on all of these but will show a couple of examples so you can see the depth.

The Dome-Shaped Table

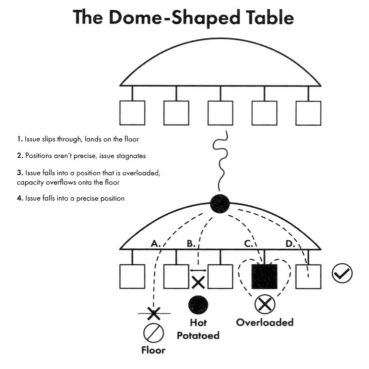

Imagine a dome-shaped table representing the organization. An issue, imagine it like a ball, lands on the table. What is it going to do? It is going to roll—the individual positions (labeled 1–4 in the image) must be precise enough to ensure the issue doesn't hit the floor, or get lost in the confusion.

I was part of the Speed Team—our Sailmaker was the lead speed guy, and I held positions on that team. The Sailmaker was also my coach.

Position: Pre-Race Prep

The purpose of pre-race prep was to work with the speed team to be sure the check list was followed and improved. All sail gear, especially gear around my Port Tack Speed duties, was ready to go. Sails were organized, inspected, and flaked; sheets were in shape and properly rigged; halyards were a go with the mast men; and winches were maintained and working. The instruments I would rely on were functioning. How was success measured? No mechanical race failures.

Position: Pre-Race Tune

The purpose of the pre-race tune was to work with the Speed Team to tune the mast and rig for the day's conditions. I would specifically man the starboard jib winch to hoist the mast man up and down the mast so he could make adjustments. I assisted the sailmaker in taking final measurements and recording these in our speed charts. Success = short-term: we are higher and faster upwind; long-term: as a Speed Team we get good at nailing the setup to the conditions we predicted.

That is enough detail, you get the picture. Other positions were:

- **Position: Pre-Race Huddle Member**

- **Position: Start**

- **Position: Port Tack Speed**

- **Position: Downwind Set** – as Port Jib Trim

- **Position: Downwind Call the Breeze** – helper to the spinnaker trimmer

- **Position: Spinnaker Douse** – as Port Jib Trim

- **Position: Post Race Speed** – as Port Jib Trim

As you can see, the pattern was around pre-race preparation, racing, then post-race review and improvement. Our positions formed a cycle of continuous improvement and communication.

The work we did in our off-water sessions with our organizational psychologist and improved during regattas was documented and recorded, and became part of the boat's OOS, passed along to the **port jib trimmer**, who followed me when I retired from the team.

It was crystal clear what was expected of me and where I fit in. The typical egos and jockeying for favor that permeated other high-dollar programs like ours were eliminated. We consistently won, as a team.

Teamwork diagram. In the accompanying diagram, note the oblong circles that link each box, or position, back to the center. The box is the particular domain of whoever holds that position, but he or she must still be linked to the center—accountable, responsible, and aware of the big picture, overall goals, etc. That center is the home of the core values and beliefs that now guide every decision. They unify team members who belong and believe. Team members have

FOR THOSE OF YOU WHO ARE FANS OF GOOGLE'S APPROACH, A GREAT WAY TO THINK ABOUT POSITIONS IS AS A STANDING/PERMANENT ORGANIZATIONAL OKR. THE PURPOSE STATEMENT IS THE OBJECTIVE, THE KEY RESULTS ARE THE SHORT-TERM AND LONG-TERM "HOW SUCCESS IS MEASURED IN NUMBERS."

I ANSWER THIS QUESTION AND HELP MY CLIENTS WORK THROUGH THIS MIND TEASER ALL THE TIME, AND ONCE THEY GET THEIR HEADS AROUND IT, IT'S VERY FREEING AND MAKES THEIR OKR APPROACH EVEN STRONGER.

increased autonomy but are accountable, no matter how far they are from the inner ring. Core values and purpose provide the torque to power a forceful waterwheel that moves independently because team members are accountable and responsible. They are being led and are not merely managed.

Teamwork Diagram

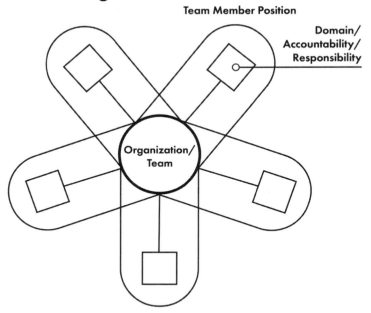

The role of your OOS is to be sure this is not a one-time exercise. ✓ Positions should be assessed all the time, at a minimum of every season. Do team members understand the amount of thinking versus doing that they should be engaged in for each position? Do they understand the boundaries of their domain and how much authority they have? Are they clear on the purpose of each position and how it relates to the overall *why*?

Position Purpose Statement Rubric

	THE PURPOSE	I FULFILL THIS PURPOSE BY	HOW SUCCESS IS MEASURED
Position A	"The purpose of position A is to . . .	"I fulfill this purpose by thinking about and being accountable for _____." "I fulfill this purpose by thinking about and being responsible for doing _____."	Long-term results that measure success are: 1. Yearly = _____ 2. Quarterly = _____ Short-term activities that drive long term success are: 1. Monthly = _____ 2. Weekly = _____ 3. Daily = _____

Position Communication Rubric

(covered deeper under "Am I Heard?")

	From my Position "A"	From my Position "B"
I report to	John Jones in Position "T"	Robert Todd in Position "S"
I am coached by	Anthony Anderson	Anthony Anderson
My peers are	My scrum mates	The CSR team
Folks I interact with internally and externally other than my problem solving peers	IT and Accounting	I take inbound calls from customers
My reports are	Suzy Q, Bobby Jones, Tommy 2 Tone	n/a
I coach	Bobby Jones, Tommy 2 Tone	n/a

Attaining and Maintaining *Yes* on Being Measured

Work on *yes*

Organization: 50%
Individual: 50%

Organization 50%	Individual 50%

PERHAPS THE BIGGEST problem with being measured is that organizations approach it as something done *to* team members. Performance evaluations, one of the most common forms of measurement that has carried forward from the Dark Ages, are generally top-down and tinged with a passive, punitive aura. Even team members who consistently get "exceeds expectations" and rave reviews grow nervous at review time, because they have as much control over and participation in the process as a film director waiting to see if her premier got panned.

I remember my four years at the "Big 8" CPA firm. I would come to the end of the year and some dude who had not even talked to me in the last six months was rating me on a rating scale/rubric I had never seen. They just popped it on me once a year with no communication during the year.

The Patient Organization wants team members to answer *yes* to the question, "Do I understand *and embrace* the ways I am measured?" I have highlighted "embrace" because that's the key piece of this puzzle what organizations almost universally neglect. If *measurement* is treated like a leash or a stick or a pat on the head, then *yes* here becomes impossible.

We need to view the whole idea of *measurement* in new terms in order to engage employees and build patience. Note that of the Seven Questions, this one is the pivot, the point at which the organization does half the work of *yes* and the individual does the other half. Typical measures, such as the performance review, place 90 to 100 percent of the burden on the organization, while the team member sits passively and, well, takes it.

Two Areas, Three Bearings

I am suggesting an approach that not only makes team members active participants in measuring, remember 50 percent of this effort, but also enlists them to help design the process. I will suggest an approach, the three-bearing, two-level rubric from each position. This is the Position Measurement Rubric (see Figure 3).

Figure 3. Position Measurement Rubric

Organizationally	Team	Individual
Position A Short Term	Position A Short Term	Position A Short Term
Position A Long Term	Position A Long Term	Position A Long Term

The two areas of measurement are 1) short-term controllable things, and 2) long-term results/outcomes that happen because we took care of the short-term controllable things. Your OOS should provide the backbone for how these are maintained, refined and communicated.✓

Let's take it back to the triangulation analogy I made earlier on. Individuals need to know how their organization measures success, how their team success is measured, and how their individual success is measured. When they are clear on their triangulated position, they can actively participate in helping define what are the best measures for themselves and their team.

If each individual has this three-bearing, two-level rubric completed for each of his or her positions, then open and honest conversations can follow, which can be employee led.

Backing up. What is a rubric? In its simplest form, it is a set of criteria that establish standards

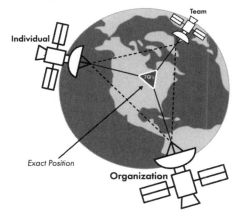

Triangulation

and concrete ways of measuring. Millennials, who will soon comprise a majority of workers, know this tool inside and out. Rubrics have become common in education, and many of your fresh workers have been using them from grade school straight through college. If you're north of forty, you might never have encountered one unless you have kids, in which case, you no doubt have poured over rubrics before helping with assignments to see what an *A* looks like, what earns a *B*, and how many points are allotted for various categories and tasks.

The rubric for a research paper, for instance, might begin with an overall purpose or learning objective and then break the assignment down into manageable segments: exercises involving sources might be worth 15 points, an outline to prepare for the paper 10, a first draft 25, and a final draft 50.

I'm not saying you get into the business of assigning points and grades. On the contrary, I'm just saying do the hard work to get agreement up front on what "good and done" looks like.

A rubric sets out measurements at a granular level before the start line. When you're given a rubric as a team member at an organization, measuring is no longer something done *to* you. Instead, the measurement itself becomes a valuable tool that provides a clear road map of what *you* must do to succeed. There is always a whiff of unfairness in performance reviews and other metrics because they come after the fact. No matter what is communicated along the way, people on some level think, "Oh, *now* you tell me."

Rubrics spell things out so clearly in advance that team members find them not just fair (rubrics are anti-SCARF on steroids) but friendly. It's hard to argue with an assessment when you agreed to the terms and criteria communicated precisely on paper before the work began. They can be the difference between metrics that

SCARF team members; one triggering a primal threat response and System 1 thinking, and another—an aid that helps them establish status, certainty, autonomy, relatedness, and fairness driving System 2 thinking.

As the millennials under your roof will attest, the more difficult or complex the work, the more comforting the rubric. Team members never need to feel that they're working in the dark or guessing what *a job well done* looks like. A rubric changes measurement from a top-down tool the organization uses on an employee after work is performed to a lateral tool used by the team member to succeed in the work. Metrics lose their element of surprise in a rubric because measuring—by team members who are now an active part of the process—also occurs every step of the way.

Is there a better way to have people understand and embrace how they're measured than by enlisting them to help design their own rubric? The process I'm encouraging is a similarly collaborative one, with responsibility for the rubric split evenly between the organization and the individual. The coach and the team member establish the key categories and weight them together. The organization takes the lead and some vital categories might be non-negotiable, but soliciting genuine input from team members gets incredible buy-in and can result in smart and creative metrics that leaders at one or several removes from the work would not have considered.

We prefer that team members own their positions. A thoughtful rubric isn't just a better way to measure, but it also defines the position with the team member's input and maps strategy. Like so many features of a Patient Organization, this one requires more work up front, but saves time and effort later, while boosting productivity. The team member with a solid rubric that he or she helped create is ready to be led, not merely managed. Over time, the organization also can use successful elements of established rubrics with new people in the same or similar positions. *This worked well with Mary. Would it work with Tom?* The process builds a treasure trove of collaterals and deep reserves of patience. ✓

HEAVY LIFT—EXERCISING PATIENCE

CREATE YOUR POSITION MEASUREMENT RUBRICS

Earlier, I provided a template you can use to begin creating rubrics of your own. This is the starting point. The idea is to think creatively with team members to design something specific to the person, position, and organization—and to reuse the successful pieces over time. Before you get started, though, here are a few reminders and general suggestions and measurement guidelines to consider.

- **Each position requires its own position measurement rubric.** I've explained why considering positions is more useful than looking at jobs, which can be made up of many positions. For the same reasons, every position should have its own rubric. Each has its own challenges, time commitments, required skills, etc., and relates to overall goals in its own way. This means one team member might be working on several rubrics at once.

- **Think long-term (or medium-term) and short-term.** Everyone must know what a touchdown looks like. The end goal should be crystal clear. But team members also must know how they are measured monthly, weekly, daily. It's important for those short-term, or leading, measures to be things within the team member's control. The long-term, or lagging, measures are shaped more by the organization, since they fit the position into an overall strategy.

- **The metrics must be understood by the whole team.** I've been talking about one-on-one collaboration, but peer meetings monthly, if not weekly, are essential. No one works in a vacuum, and the organization's 50 percent share of *yes* on measuring includes team input.

- **Customize rubrics to individuals.** Within reason, try to include or emphasize categories that will motivate the particular team member working off the rubric. Quotas never worked for me. But for other people, they're lifeblood. Can the rubric be tweaked to reflect whatever best motivates the individual?

- **Be creative.** Soliciting input from team members, think about categories that might be helpful for them beyond the obvious measures. This might include changing a habit, developing a routine, or starting on something they've avoided.

- **Work your core values and *why* into every rubric.** These are the lenses through which we view everything at a Patient Organization, and they need to be a part of this patient tool.

- **Use the seasonal meeting to keep it sharp.** ✓ This one-on-one is the time to go over the rubric with team members, mark progress, and assess how they're doing in various categories.

Attaining and Maintaining *Yes* on Being Heard

Work on *yes*

Organization: 30%
Individual: 70%

MY COACH, GREG Walker, reminds me constantly of this fact: Folks are always tuned to their own personal internal channel—WIIFM—What's In It For Me. Don't forget that.

If you don't feel that you're being heard, why toss out a fresh idea? Why point out inefficiencies that could be corrected, or suggest a new process? Why mention the things that would make you more engaged or productive at work? Why say anything at all unless it's in response to direct questions?

People need to feel that they're being heard in order to get anywhere, which is why getting team members to say *yes* to the question, *Do I understand and embrace how I am heard?* is vital. Not being heard, whether it's because people don't have the patience to listen or because the channels of communication are inadequate, not only hurts the individual's engagement, but it also stymies the organization by smothering innovation, stifling feedback, and crippling collaboration.

For team members to feel that they're being heard, leaders must learn to actively listen. Obvious, right? I agree, but that does not make the act of listening any easier inside an organization with as many personality types as there are team members, as many problems to solve as there are hours in the day, as many deadlines as there are days. Listening in the midst of what the 4DX Organizational Operating System calls "the whirlwind," the daily exigencies of work, requires time and effort. Perhaps most of all, it requires patience. It is the job of your OOS to install and maintain the organization's methods for hearing. ✓

When I ask people what the word *patience* brings to mind (I've spent a lot of time asking that question in recent years), some version of listening, hearing, good listener, etc., tops the list. You cannot become a Patient Organization without listening to your members— all of them—and getting them to embrace the ways they are heard, and how and when the organization listens is the job of your OOS. ✓

Each of the 7Qs requires that people are *heard*. If you need certain skills to *belong*, will someone listen as you explain the deficit and help you acquire those skills? (Nodding with a sympathetic smile is not *hearing* if you immediately forget what was just said or do nothing about it.) If you don't understand how parts of an announced strategy align with the organization's *why*, is there a channel that allows you to express that concern? Is your feedback on rubrics *heard* in ways that help you buy in and say *yes* on *measurement*? As we'll explore, the last two of the Seven Questions, on balance and development, require individuals to do the heavy lifting, but that's impossible if they are speaking in a vacuum. Sound does not travel in a vacuum. There must exist a medium for sound to travel; it is up to your OOS to lay down how the organization listens. ✓

This question about being heard is the first of the seven where most of the work falls on the individual, around 70 percent. The organization, however, must address its 30 percent of the effort before the individual can work on his or her share. Clear channels, mechanisms, and strategies that allow for true hearing must be established. For people to be heard, the channels must be two-way, not simply top-down. This also sounds obvious, I realize, and yet every organization I've encountered needs work in this area. ✓

As Lencioni argues, the basis for embracing the effort it takes to be heard is *trust*[16]—and the way to build trust is by maintaining *yes* to the Seven Questions. I'll explore this more later, but first, I want to return yet again to language, the basic building block of human communication.

Language, I have argued, is what allows humans to come together in groups to solve complex problems. The conference call, email thread, and Skype session are modern versions of tribal elders passing the talking stick around the fire outside the cave. We are social animals that, over eons, evolved with language. It's embedded in our brains, but the technological progress that has moved us forward has also been a step back in some ways.

Text-based electronic communication is necessary and efficient, but it removes a layer of perception that evolved over millions of years to help humans survive. Communicating through a device is a little like having a conversation in noise-cancelling headphones while listening to your favorite book in the background. You'll hear most words, but you've dulled a few key senses. Have you ever attempted

---

16   Patrick Lencioni, *The Five Dysfunctions of a Team: A Leadership Fable* (Hoboken: Jossey-Bass, 2002).

a joke on email that fell flat, was taken as serious, or worse, offended someone, though your intentions were innocent? The exact same words uttered face-to-face are much less likely to be misread, partly because tone and expression of voice, and body language, tell us so much. The static zeros and ones that make it to our screens are miraculous, but are no equal for the nuance of a human voice, which we react to biologically in endless, important ways.

Phone calls, of course, involve a clear human voice. They must be just as good as meeting in person, right? Not really. Much like tone of voice, facial expressions and body language convey immense amounts of data. Research has shown that much, perhaps most, information processing occurs in the brain with no accompanying conscious experience. Some of the processing becomes conscious later, but much of it influences perception and behavior without our awareness.[17]

Many of our judgements based on facial expressions and features—even those glimpsed in milliseconds—prove surprisingly accurate. Research has shown that this includes things that would seem impossible to predict, including how much money a CEO will make for the company in a given year and the leadership skills of executives as measured in bottom-line profits.[18] Most of us understand that we have a better sense of skepticism or enthusiasm or slight hesitancy when we see a face reacting, or a head nod, but that's only the tip of the iceberg. Our brains are processing massive amounts of

---

17   Daniel E. Re and Nicholas O. Rule, "Predicting Firm Success From the Facial Appearance of Chief Executive Officers of Non-Profit Organizations," Perception 45, no. 10 (October 2016): 1137–1150, https://doi.org/10.1177/0301006616652043

18   Ibid.

data and important nuances every minute that we're with another human.

My advice when it comes to upping effective communication is to *Go Verbal*—a phrase I coined and use all the time with my clients—whenever possible. By this I don't mean just a phone call, but real voices emanating from real bodies in the same room. There is no substitute for this kind of human interaction when it comes to being fully heard and listening actively. Of course, email, texting, calls, and video conferences have their uses, but how often these days are we trading emails with someone down the hall when a quick face-to-face would actually take less time? Such interactions are richer and through them, our primal SCARF needs are more likely to be met. I think most of us would agree that our feelings of status, certainty, and relatedness, in particular, are richer when we're looking someone in the eye.

Meetings are the most common way of *going verbal* in organizations. The most important meeting for *yes* on being heard, and on all of the Seven Questions, is the 7Qs Yeses Seasonal Meeting. I will hit this hard under *Developed*. This one-on-one reset is a chance for a team member to go over rubrics with their coach, and to see how well they as individuals are aligned with core values and the organization's *why*. It is also a chance to listen as the team member assesses whether he or she is at *yes* on the Seven Questions.

Meetings are an indispensable extension of our tribal roots, but they also provide ample evidence that *going verbal* is no guarantee that people will be heard. In Part II, I explored some of the ways meetings tend to drift. They start or run late. They have the wrong names, weak agendas, unclear objectives, poor focus, or the wrong attendees. All are items your OOS should handle and address.

An important part of *yes* to being *heard* involves finding the right rhythm for your meetings. That process starts with deciding on the type of meeting you're scheduling and is the bailiwick of your OOS.✓ Earlier, I discussed the two main categories as defined by Michael Gerber, author of *The E-Myth*, the *in* meetings, which discuss daily work, tasks, and problems, and *on* meetings, which rise above daily and monthly concerns to focus on systemic issues, long-term goals, and the future of the business. Deciding whether meetings are *in* or *on* is a great way to begin focusing them. If it's an *in* meeting, don't drift off into a discussion of the three-year plan—the immediate problems won't get solved. Likewise, don't let the *on* meeting get hijacked by this week's sluggish sales. Again, this is the job of your OOS to challenge the structures of your meetings.

It's also helpful, after you consider Gerber's broad classification, to get more specific. Is this an informational meeting, called solely to convey data, news, or procedures? If so, then the 80-20 rule might be in effect: the leader or facilitator will speak around 80 percent of the time, and the remaining 20 percent will be Q&A.✓ If it's a brainstorming meeting, the format might be looser, with speaking time divided fairly evenly around the room. Your OOS should be the guide to making decisions around your types and timing.

The problem-solving meeting, the quarterly sales meeting, the strategic-planning meeting—every type has its own flavor, shaped by objectives, but the following elements are key to making all meetings good channels of communication:✓

- **Objective.** Every meeting should have a clear objective, or focus becomes impossible.

- **Agenda.** Every meeting should have a distributed agenda that leaders stick to. As tangents arise, identify them—

tangent alert!—and decide if they warrant their own meetings.

- **Name.** I've written enough about the importance of language by now that I don't need say that how we name meetings is important. Labels shape expectations and attitudes.

- **One channel.** Everyone in the meeting should be tuned into the same channel, which ultimately, is WIIFM. Too often, the marketing guy zones out at the sales meeting he shouldn't be attending, while the salespeople are tuned in.

- **Core values and your why.** Every meeting should look at choices, problems, and issues through the lens of organizational core values and *why* for all the reasons explored in the section on getting to *yes* on belonging and believing.

- **No minutes.** Many will disagree with me, but I believe that a meeting that requires minutes has failed. If people are communicating well and engaged, it all gets covered in the meeting. Minutes are not necessary.

- **Big ears.** Are leaders doing all the talking? They should be listening actively and leading with questions when they can.

- **Trust.** People will never get to *yes* on embracing how they're heard without trust. Organizations must create an atmosphere where people feel safe speaking up, asking questions, raising objections, testing ideas, and generally making themselves vulnerable. (Read *The Five Dysfunctions of a Team* by Patrick Lencioni.)

- **Ratings**. Gino Wickman, creator of EOS®, advises that you rate your meetings. On a scale of 1–10, how helpful was this meeting? Did we stay on track? Did we stick to the agenda? Such a rating in itself can become an important channel for people to feel heard, and it will make for better meetings.

Patrick Lencioni, in *Five Dysfunctions of a Team*, talks about great meetings and team work in terms of a pyramid, with trust as the foundation. This allows people to be honest and vulnerable, he says, and to focus on issues, not egos. He's absolutely right that trust is the foundation, but the question then becomes, how do you build trust? The answer, I have found through my years of experience and research, is by alignment with *yes* to the Seven Questions. People who belong and believe, and can answer *yes* on accountability, measurement, hearing, development, and balance have a deep reserve of trust in themselves, their leaders, each other, and the organization.

HEAVY LIFT—EXERCISING PATIENCE

GET YOUR HEARING TESTED, EXPERIMENT WITH *GO VERBAL*

One way to begin helping team members understand and embrace *yes* on being heard is by *going verbal*—communicating face-to-face whenever possible. How *verbal* is your team?

Find out. Choose a date and call it Communication Day—an average Tuesday or Wednesday will do. Have everyone at the organization log every interaction during the workday, noting how long it lasted and the medium it occurred through (in-person conversation, phone, email, etc.). Ask people to calculate the percentage of time they spent on each form of communication and then tally the organization-wide totals to share with all team members. What can you learn from the results? Are there any correlations between those who seem most successful or productive and the percentage of time they spend communicating in a particular way? Are there any connections between those who seem to have communication issues and their reliance on a particular medium? To take it further, tell staff that during the next month, you would like them—within reason and without interrupting workflow—to communicate in person whenever possible. Release the Velcro holding you to your seat and pop over to talk to Tim in accounting to discuss a client who stopped paying invoices rather than trading four emails. Visit HR with your benefits questions rather than dialing the extension. Near the end of the month, take another tally. How much, if at all, has the percentage of face-to-face conversation risen? Solicit feedback from team members. What did they think of the experiment? How, if at all, did it affect their work quality, productivity, or sense of belonging and believing? Have leaders noticed any marked improvements or drop-offs as a result of the change?

HEAVY LIFT—EXERCISING PATIENCE

TAKE A MEETING INVENTORY EACH SEASON: A JOB FOR YOUR OOS ✔

I am obviously a big fan of meeting face-to-face, but I am not encouraging pointless meetings. We have plenty of those already. At some organizations, meetings proliferate like rabbits, and team members come to dread them. They become a major suck on time and energy, creating more problems than they solve.

How do we avoid this? Just as team members need a reset every ninety days, so too does the meeting schedule. Your OOS should complete an ad hoc meeting inventory once each season. List every meeting that's taking place at the organization and examine the following areas, with an eye to cutting superfluous meetings whenever possible:

- **Name.** Are all meetings named correctly? Sometimes a tack (tack is a sailing term, normally around 90-degrees from where you were headed) on the label can change emphasis, making the meeting more productive or focused.

- **Utility.** Do all the meetings on your list need to stay? They have a way of lingering beyond their usefulness once they get on the schedule. The meeting that made sense last quarter might now be unnecessary. What can be scrapped?

- **Frequency.** Are there meetings occurring monthly that could be held quarterly and produce the same results? Can a weekly meeting happen biweekly?

- **Attendance.** Are all the right people in all the right meetings? Frequently, team members get included in meetings they don't need to attend. Have coaches ask during seasonal one-on-ones what meetings team members are going to. Are there any they think they could skip?

- **Feedback.** Have someone tally and summarize the ratings team members have given the meetings they attended all season. What trends emerge? Can a meeting that receives low marks be improved or scrapped? What can you replicate from the meetings that get the most positive feedback?

REVIEW AND UPDATE EACH INDIVIDUAL'S POSITION COMMUNICATION RUBRIC

Here we are getting super-clear triangulation for each individual across six bearings, they answer: 1) this is who I report to, 2) this is who I am coached by (yes, might be different), 3) my peers are (meaning the teams you meet with), 4) I interact with (these are the internal or external folks you communicate with that are not necessarily on your team; customers, other departments, people you impact), 5) my direct reports are, and 6) the folks I coach are.

Using this easy to follow visual rubric is a great way to understand communication loads *(See next page)*.

Position and Communications Rubric

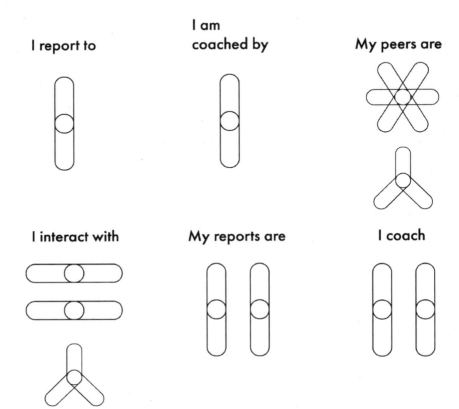

I report to

I am
coached by

My peers are

I interact with

My reports are

I coach

	From my Position "A"	From my Position "B"
I report to	John Jones in Position "T"	Robert Todd in Position "S"
I am coached by	Anthony Anderson	Anthony Anderson
My peers are	My scrum mates	The CSR team
Folks I interact with internally and externally other than my problem solving peers	IT and Accounting	I take inbound calls from customers
My reports are	Suzy Q, Bobby Jones, Tommy 2 Tone	n/a
I coach	Bobby Jones, Tommy 2 Tone	n/a

Attaining and Maintaining *Yes* on Development

Work on *yes*

Organization: 20%
Individual: 80%

MOST TEAM MEMBERS want to develop, and if a path for their development isn't clear, the organization is likely to lose them. As I discussed in Part II, *development* might involve a class, a certification, a conference, or safety training, but it also could include changing a habit, meeting regularly with a coach, or taking on a new position.

These, however, are tactics. Such efforts need to exist in support of clear strategies that help realize long-term future-based development goals.✓ People want development, but, often, not the hard work it requires, just as many of us want to get fit but find reasons to avoid the gym. It's easy to rationalize putting off certification on a new machine or the time commitment of an evening class when you have a busy workday. Development requires patience, and the organization can cultivate it by helping team members to turn their attention to their futures.

The organization's active role here is relatively small—perhaps 20 percent of the effort—but important and should be mapped by your OOS. The other 80 percent of the effort is truly up to the individual whose effort will be directly influenced by three factors.

Three Development Influencers

There are three areas that influence one's commitment to their own development—again a triangulation: 1) there is the organization or tribe, 2) there is the team or family, and 3) there is the individual or self. Tribe, Family, Self, if we keep the ancestral metaphor moving.

Tribally, one's development will be influenced by the idea of swimming with the current or against the current, the job of the OOS for the organization is to clearly set and communicate this current's direction so the individual can understand if they are motivated, neutral, or demotivated by it: simple but super important. Going to work and swimming against the current of where you imagine your future to be is exhausting and cannot be maintained. The tribe is migrating, it is going to be cold and hard, do you want to come along? Yes or No?

One's work family or team has more impact on development than we often acknowledge; this is where the on-the-job training happens. Keeping with the family metaphor, I use the acronym "EATT": in order to survive, families and organizations must Evolve; in order to evolve, they must Adapt; and in order to adapt, they must Trust and Try (figure out what and why something works). The role of a family or team in the development of the individual is to create the team trying events as part of the natural flow of work. Teams are the best at seeing what is working and what is not working, and they are best at determining what we will try next—from this determination, teammates are given opportunities to EATT—it is not something truly planned for the individual, it just happens as the normal part of teamwork. Your OOS plays a part in this on the job (OTJ) development. In the world of EOS® and Rockefeller Habits, they use short-term Rocks (top three to five priorities); 4DX extracts short-term goals out of what they call The Whirlwind, via a team meeting they call the WIG Session—WIG standing for "Wildly Important Goals." Rocks and WIGs are owned by individuals and are typically things a bit outside of the normal day—trying things that drives adaptation, which helps the organization and individual to evolve. The team leader is the one accountable for driving the EATT pattern. Get this type of rotation moving in your organization, and the water-wheel will turn from the weight of your individuals developing.

A QUICK ASIDE ABOUT WHAT THIS TEAM LEADER MUST BE. 4AS—ALIGNED, ACCOUNTABLE, AUTHENTIC, AND AWARE. IN ORDER TO LEAD, EACH TEAM MEMBER MUST SEE YOU, THEIR LEADER AS ALIGNED TO THE OVERALL GOOD, ACCOUNTABLE—DOING WHAT YOU SAY YOU ARE GOING TO DO, AUTHENTIC—YOU ARE NOT PRETENDING, ARE HONEST ABOUT YOURSELF, AND YOU ARE AWARE—NOT DULL WITTED, DEAF, PRETENDING TO HEAR, NOT HEARING. THESE FOUR WORDS ARE A MASH UP OF THE WORK OF DR. COVEY'S SPEED OF TRUST AND DR. JOHN GRINNELL'S BEYOND BELIEF. IF YOU ARE FAKING IT IN ANY OF THESE 4AS, YOUR FOLKS WILL SMELL IT AND WILL NOT COMMIT TO FOLLOW.

A quick aside about what this team leader must be. 4As—Aligned, Accountable, Authentic, and Aware. In order to lead, each team member must see you, their leader as aligned to the overall good, accountable—doing what you say you are going to do, authentic— you are not pretending, are honest about yourself, and you are aware—not dull witted, deaf, pretending to hear, not hearing. These four words are a mash up of the work of Dr. Covey's Speed of Trust and Dr. John Grinnell's Beyond Belief.[19] If you are faking it in any of these 4As, your folks will smell it and will not commit to follow.

The third influencer is one's imagined future self/WIIFM. Remember SCARF as it relates to a tribe, humans are motivated by the future and just need help going into that future and mapping a path back to the present touching the SCARF stepping stones along the way. Some folks are natural future people. "Futuristic" is one of Gallup's strength-finders strengths, and this type of person is driven to see their future and map a path to it. However, most people do not have this gene baked in and need assistance—they are still very motivated by the future, they just need help being a part of it.

In fact, as I mentioned in Part II, answering *yes* to the Seven Questions should organically produce a development path and awareness of one's future. If team members understand and embrace the organization's core values and *why*, if they are accountable and embrace how they're measured, they understand how their organization listens and how they are heard, then they should be able to develop the goals they need to work toward their imagined futures. Figuring out what's needed to achieve these goals to a large extent becomes their development program and requires a coach.

"Two lives working on one." This is the definition of what coaching is. A coach has a natural desire to give of self for the benefit

---

19   Stephen M. R. Covey, *Speed of Trust: The One Thing That Changes Everything* (New York: Simon & Schuster, 2008); John Grinnell, *Beyond Belief: Awaken Potential, Focus Leadership* (Promethean-Mind Media, 2014).

of another. A coach brings a methodical and consistent approach so the effort is focused. Imagine using the 7Qs as a way to drive open and honest two lives working on one conversations to enable individuals to imagine their futures and map a path to it.

The coach who huddles with the team member as part of what I often call "two lives working on one" can use the 7Q *Yeses* to ascertain the individual's long-term goals, help with strategies for getting there, and brainstorm tactics that will achieve the strategies. The tactics become more palatable when they're part of a patient approach focused on a larger goal that might be one or several years out and is clearly aligned with the organization's *why*.

The coach and team are a catalyst or enabler, but the individual ideally does 80 percent of the work on development. Humans are more motivated when they have autonomy, and this is especially true in development. Also, on a practical level, leaders live in a core that might be several orbital layers removed from the work that various team members are doing. The individuals are the ones immersed in the work in their Organizational Orbit (see figure), perhaps four or five rings out. If we want them to own their position, then they must also own the procedures and processes that support it. Giving them the authority to refine those processes feeds development and underpins autonomy. The team member knows better than anyone where his or her gaps, talents, and potential paths forward lie. The role of your OOS is to codify and systemize how these development efforts happen and are maintained, it is not the sole domain of HR.

Organizational Orbits

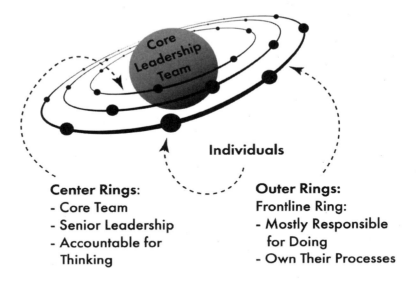

Center Rings:
- Core Team
- Senior Leadership
- Accountable for Thinking

Outer Rings:
Frontline Ring:
- Mostly Responsible for Doing
- Own Their Processes

HEAVY LIFT—EXERCISING PATIENCE

THE SEASONAL 7 *YESES* MEETING

The Seasonal Meeting is ground-zero for development, and the rubrics used for measurement and accountability are important tools for this question. Because the rubric is concrete and specific, it can be incorporated into a development plan. Jim might be doing well in most areas, but on copyrighting—one of several smaller but important positions he occupies—he is falling short. In particular, he's losing "points" for clarity, organization, and color—specific measurement categories on the rubric for how he is to fulfill the purpose of this position. At his suggestion, we're signing him up for an online editing course and he's meeting weekly with Debbie, our best copywriter, for the next ninety days to get feedback on his writing.

In this case, the coach might be collaborating with Jim on his overall goal of versatility: within three years, Jim wants to be proficient in every marketing position in the department, not just social media, which is his specialty. Together, he and his coach discuss a strategy of gradually pushing boundaries and improving his skills for a different position every six months. The online course and meetings with Debbie are tactics that help him realize the strategy.

Coach v. Team Lead. While often one's coach is also the team lead or someone you report to, this is not always the case. In really functional organizations, I often see player coaches, people who are part of a person's team, but not necessarily the official team leader, filling the role of coach. These coaches are often very skilled at their work and are super-talented at tutoring, yet, are not pulled to "lead" a team. They can detach their egos, see value in helping for the overall good first, by helping those around them. Coaching for this type of person is highly rewarding.

THIS DEVELOPMENT WORK BUILDS PATIENCE AND THE TEMPLATES TO SCALE

Just as rubrics should be customized to the person as well as the position when possible, so development must be tailored to the individual. Not everyone learns at the same pace or in the same ways, as I pointed out in Part II. Putting the team member in charge of his or her own development paves the most effective path forward. We are not so different, however, that big pieces of an organic development program can't provide templates for other team members in similar positions. When, next year, Nancy is struggling in her copyrighting duties, her coach can say, well, here are the steps that worked for Jim. This becomes a key part of your scalability—development templates possibly captured in the form of Rocks or WIGs, to use words from EOS®, Rockefeller Habits, and 4DX.

A final caveat before I move on to structuring seasonal meetings: not everyone wants more than the bare minimum of development. As I have mentioned, there's no point in forcing an ambitious development program on the coal cars who are happy where they are. This is yet another reason that the team member should take the lead in his or her own development.

My colleagues always seem a little mystified and amazed when Gino Wickman, the creator of EOS®, shrugs his shoulders and wiggles a little saying: *Humans just sort of get off track every ninety days—I don't know why, they just do.* Gino is right. Having grown up on and around my grandfather's farm, and running a super-seasonal company for twenty years, I'm not at all mystified. Ninety days, or three months, is a season, and seasons have provided the natural rhythm that shaped how humans ate, lived, and planned for millions of years. The natural division of seasons is a part of our tribal roots and embedded in our DNA. Organizations can harness that natural cadence by making the **7 Yeses Seasonal** Meeting a cornerstone of team member alignment and development.

Seasonal meetings were baked into our world at Layline. Remember, we sold stuff to households that raced sailboats and showed horses. These are seasonal selling activities coupled with seasonal style changes. These changes forced us to have seasonal meetings with each team member just to stay aligned with the work of a year. In the fall, Chief would be in charge of spring summer selections and horseshows in Florida; in the winter, she would be choosing the next fall and winter selection and getting the catalogs and websites aligned. In the spring and summer seasons, she was in charge of selling and running the summer shows in the northeast. We were so seasonal that we could not afford to do without our seasonal meetings: they were how we stayed aligned.

I have mentioned the **7 Yeses Seasonal** Meeting in reference to each of the Seven Questions. It is a cornerstone tool of an effective OOS and for aligning and maintaining *yes* on all of the Seven Questions, not just *development*. Your OOS should recommend scheduling a seasonal meeting for every team member of the organization. On an intuitive, even biological, basis, people will appreciate the way it structures their year and use it as a marker to measure progress on development as well as alignment with the organization's core values and *why.*

The one-on-one seasonal meeting is the time to go over rubrics and make sure people are maintaining a *yes* on Accountability. The agenda for this meeting is the 7Qs, and it is led by the team member, who has helped create her own rubric. The coach who meets with the team member gives feedback on every category on the rubric, but it's most important that people are measuring themselves, highlighting strengths, detailing impediments on the road to *yes,* and creating strategies for development. This meeting is one of the chief mechanisms for *yes* on being heard, but that's not possible if the coach does all the talking. ✓

The most simple rubric/meeting agenda looks like this *(see next page)*:

I EMBRACE AND UNDERSTAND HOW	YES	NO
I Belong		
I Believe		
I am Accountable		
I am Measured		
I am Heard		
I am Developed		
I am Balanced		

The **7 Yeses Seasonal** Meeting will have different elements depending on the organization, but here are some general guidelines for structuring this invaluable tool:

- **Coach.** The meeting must have a coach. The person meeting with the team member might be a supervisor, team leader, or mentor, but I encourage you to think of him or her as coaching—pointing out strengths and areas that need work, and helping with a development plan. One of the most important parts of this position is simply listening. Refer to two lives working on one above.

- **Schedule.** This can't be an ad hoc or random meeting. It must be on the schedule.

- **Employee Lead.** Team members run this meeting and should expect it and prepare for it; it is employee led. They need to know that the Seven Questions will come up.

- **Rubrics.** Like the 7Qs rubric above, other organizational rubrics are an important organizational tool for these meetings. Team members should expect to assess every area on their rubrics, talk about ways they've improved, highlight deficits, and adjust development plans. The coach will offer his or her own assessments in each area, but it's best to let the team member own the position and lead the discussion.

- **Positions.** Clarity on how the organization captures positions is part of every OOS, and the team members must bring this with them. For this to be an effective meeting, team members must understand their positions and what they are accountable for thinking and responsible for doing all day. This is the time to connect the purpose of their positions with the larger organizational purpose. Simon Sinek's Golden Circle can be a helpful model here.

Attaining and Maintaining *Yes* on Balance

Work on *yes*

Organization: 20%
Individual: 80%

IN PART II, I discussed balance mostly as a way to help people negotiate the demands of work and life. This is an important aspect of Question 7, but not the only one. In a broader sense, *balance* also is about making sure that team members have the most productive day possible. Part of that effort means making allowances for the demands of life outside of work, but it also involves carving out space and time for thought at work.

Keeping people chained to phones and emails every minute of the day can look highly productive at first glance, but, in fact, it's a way to kill productivity. Especially in positions that require thinking and not just doing, team members need time to step back, rise above the daily work, and strategize. Leaders unwittingly encourage simplistic System 1 thinking with pressure or workloads so intense that team members feel that they're living under constant threat, SCARFed on a daily basis. They don't have the time to pause in order to consider a better process or the flaws in a system if they're too entangled in it to see it clearly.

Organizations that neglect balance in this way create busy fools, always rushing from one fire to the next. The organization that helps team members say, *yes, I have Balance,* creates an environment that is proactive, not reactive. Allowing the space for balance, however, requires patience on the part of leaders. Most organizations see time as money, so letting people carve out time to just think, time off for family issues, or an hour for that important daily workout comes at a cost. Part of becoming a Patient Organization is realizing that this cost pays high dividends in productivity, sharper System 2 thinking, anti-SCARF, and loyalty.

Most of the work of *yes* on *balance* falls on the individual, around 80 percent. Only team members can fully appreciate the demands they're facing on and off the job, so it's up to them to bring up the issues, suggest what they need, and work at achieving balance.

Three Balance Influencers

Exactly like development, there are three areas that influence one's commitment to their own balance—again a triangulation—1) the organization or tribe, 2) the team or family, and 3) the individual or self. Tribe, Family, Self, if we keep the ancestral metaphor moving.

Tribally, the organization must be very frank and clear about its work expectations. A CPA firm must be very clear that during the busy season, the firm will own you eighty hours per week. A retailer like Layline who has a busy season must be very clear that we do not think about leaving until the last customer is served and that we open on time.

As a team, *sharing of the load* and *for the greater good* are the key phrases here. A team must be aware of the talents/unique abilities of each teammate and help guide those unique abilities against the needs and priorities of the team. The team leader must demonstrate the 4As—Aligned, Accountable, Authentic, and Aware—not only thinking about themselves but helping the entire team be aligned, accountable, authentic and aware as they orient to the overall good. When each team member views their own teammates as being 4A, then open discussions around work load balance become natural and ongoing.

For the individual, the organization should make space for agreement and discussion around balance, ideally during a seasonal meeting with a coach. As I highlighted in Part II, the priority for the coach is openness. *Here is what we are agreeing you're accountable for, here is how we are agreeing you will be measured. Are we in agreement?* I prefer "agreement" over "expectation" in this discussion because, as author Steve Chandler points out, expectations leave too much implied. They're one-sided, top-down, and lead to disappointment. Agreement is fifty-fifty, with equal buy-in and commitment on both sides.[20]

HEAVY LIFT 1.—EXERCISING PATIENCE

FIND YOUR BALANCE

Yes on *balance* requires high levels of trust and honesty. If SCARF needs have been neglected, then the kinds of conversations that help team members find balance become impossible. Working through

---

20   Steve Chandler, "Choices for a More Powerful You," http://www.stevechandler.com/choices.html.

the previous six questions is the best way to build trust and encourage honesty.

THINK ABOUT BALANCE CONSIDERING THESE THOUGHTS.

Here are some practical things to consider as team members work to get to *yes* on balance, these should be driven by your OOS:✔

- **Belong and believe.** Is the balance between work and life that the organization allows honestly conveyed in its core values, and why? If staying until the last customer is served or working eighty-hour weeks at crunch time is a vital part of who you are, communicate that through core values, your why, policies, positions, so people can determine if your balance is right for them.

- **Open conversations.** It makes the HR department nervous, but during the seasonal meeting, ask team members about their lives and plans outside of work. If Pat is thirty-two and got married three years ago, it's quite possible Pat is considering starting a family. Is that something Pat and the organization should plan for?

- **Check the diaper.** Nine out of ten times, a bad attitude, drop-off in productivity, or misalignment with core values is the result of some outside pressure—a sick child, a divorce, an alcohol addiction, financial problems, etc. For children, my mother-in-law would say "look to the physical first." In other words, just be aware—what unpleasant stuff is someone carrying around that is making them unbalanced, miserable? Simply by paying attention, asking if something is wrong, asking what's going on, and letting a team member know that the organization cares creates immense good will, and, more importantly, an awareness of how we can reestablish balance. If we cannot see what is on the scale, it is impossible to balance that scale.

- **Accountability.** The assessment of all positions as part of getting to *yes* on Question 3 is a chance to restore balance for team members who might have found themselves helping out in areas not their own, or, have found themselves occupying too many positions. Open conversations around this is the only way to find balance.

- **Communication.** Electronic interference in the form of endless emails, texts, and memos is frequently an obstacle to balance. I call this our *electronic leash*. Going verbal can help address this. Offsite meetings, away from office distractions, will help leadership, too. A former client of mine established the "no-email hour" from 10:45 to 11:45 every morning to boost focus and carve out space for higher-level thinking. We could call this the Patient Hour.

- **Policies.** As I said in Part II, it's important to be clear about the organization's policies on leave, sick days, benefits, etc. If they're on the books, they should be honored without hesitation. If a team member can't find balance within these parameters, he's at the wrong organization.

- **Leading.** Merely managing people destroys balance. Leading them with the 4As (alignment, accountability, authenticity, and awareness) and working for and maintaining *yes* on the Seven Questions provides the autonomy they desire. It's much easier for a team member who is being led and has autonomy to find balance.

A SIMPLE BALANCE SURVEY

A simple survey is also a good way to get the team thinking about things that throw them off balance, and to get the organization thinking about systemic changes that might improve it. Throwing in a survey makes the discussion of balance at the seasonal meeting more productive, too. Below are some sample questions to get you started. Have team members answer the following on a scale of 1–10 in writing:

- Does the organization grant enough space for higher-level thinking about my positions?

- Does my work leave adequate room for life outside of work?

- Do I feel guilty when I take time off?

- Is the organization honest about time commitments and the balance it allows between work and life?

- Are policies regarding time off, sick leave, mental health, etc., conveyed clearly and administered fairly?

- When is the last time I had a conversation with a coach or leader about challenges I'm facing outside of work and how they might affect it? 1 = never, 10 = open conversation.

KEEP IT SIMPLE—USE THE SEVEN QUESTIONS

"I AM HELPING Sir Christopher Wrenn Build Saint Paul's Cathedral."

Our mason back in Chapter 1, with this simple response, answered *yes* to the Seven Questions. It can be that simple.

How?

Go Verbal, Make a Promise

Go verbal and make a promise to each person under your roof and to your organization as a whole: *Everyone, I am making a promise to you. We are going to build a Patient Organization. I am promising to surround you with these types of people. These are our core values. This is our* why. *I want you to be able to answer* yes *to these Seven Questions, and here is how we go about that.*

A simple, constantly repeated, verbal promise is a powerful psychological human tool. When we say something, and then repeat it often, it has a tendency to come true, and we hold ourselves to a higher standard.

Most entrepreneurs have a dream before they have a business. I began writing this book by talking about that dream, the innovative product someone knew he or she could deliver, the smart organization someone was sure he or she could create, the superior service that would leave the competition stunned.

People were always at the center of that dream—smart and talented, sure, but more than that, these are the people you imagine when you set out to start an organization shared your core values, whether or not you called them that. They shared your purpose and were, quite simply, people you wanted to spend time with.

What happened? How did the people who don't really belong or believe creep in? Where did the daily dysfunction come from? Where did the dream go?

Don't worry, it's still there. Virtually all of your problems, as I've said throughout this book, are people problems, and the dream is alive and well beneath them. People are complex animals. If there's a gap between your original dream and the current organization, it likely exists because your systems for dealing with people—communicating with them, measuring them, managing, and leading them, etc.—aren't adequate.

Management techniques never are. The headaches, dysfunction, and lack of focus you're facing are common. Management treats organizations and their members like soulless machines. It tends to ignore human psychology, social dynamics, even biology, to impose order from on high. It is built according to profits and efficiency. I'm all for both—they're the ultimate result of what I do—but the best way to address profits and efficiency, paradoxically, is to start with the needs of the human beings that make up the team, the organization.

What do the humans who *are* the organization want? (Remember, an organization is essentially a fiction that dies if enough people stop believing in it.) They want to be *led,* not managed. They want to belong and believe, to be truly accountable. They want to know that they are being measured fairly and that their opinions are heard. They want to develop and crave balance.

Answering *yes* to the Seven Questions can resurrect and achieve the dream. There are only seven of them, and, together, they cover all your team members' concerns, but as you know by now, getting to and maintaining *yes* is tough. It takes time and effort, and if done correctly, it will inflict pain. The end of this book is just the beginning.

Don't panic. Panic is the opposite of patience, and patience is the goal here. Don't make this harder than it has to be. The 7Qs rest on common sense, and that should be your guide. Follow the steps in Part III. Start by deciding on your core values and create a Belief statement. *Go verbal* and make a promise to each person under your roof: *We are trying to build a Patient Organization. These are our core values. This is our* why. *We want you to be able to answer* yes *to these Seven Questions, and here is* how *we go about that.*

Determine Where You Are Now

The Seven Questions Inventory is a short survey that walks team members through the Seven Questions, asking them to answer each by rating on a simple scale how close they are to *yes.* This is a great way to kick off the promise with team members, gauge how much work lies ahead, and begin forming a strategy. Find it over at: www.ThePatientOrganization.com.

Take Inventory of Your Organizational Operating System

The Seven Questions themselves are the best for this purpose—and will help you assess whether or not your current OOS is adequate. A good OOS should get you to *yes* on all Seven Questions. Some are quite good overall but leave gaps in certain areas. The gaps must be patched, or the organization suffers. If you developed an OOS yourself, organically, does it get you to *yes* on the Seven Questions? If so, they can be overlaid seamlessly onto your OOS to build patience in the organization. If not, the 7Qs will highlight where your OOS is falling short. Can it be improved or should you consider installing a prepackaged OOS?

Any OOS can be customized to fit your organization—that's the whole idea—and the pace will also vary, depending on the facts on the ground. Some leaders can honestly say, *yes, we are two years into a core values initiative, and we have thought deeply about our purpose.* They might need work on accountability and measurement, but be close to *yes* in most areas. Others perhaps have never thought seriously about incorporating core values into the organization, and they face a longer road.

After you have analyzed your OOS fit to the 7Qs, think of the tools you must develop and include into your OOS to get the team to *yes*. How will you structure your seasonal meeting? What will your rubric look like? There is no need to reinvent the wheel here. Visit my website, www.ThePatientOrganization.com, and you will find an inventory of links to tools from various OOSs and OOS thinkers that you can use as part of your OOS.

Be Patient

Whatever your status, transformation does not happen quickly. A strong effort in my experience takes eighteen months to bear fruit, and three years to fully implement. The effort doesn't end in three years, of course—in a sense, it never ends. The organization is always striving to get people to *yes* and to maintain it, to keep filling the buckets that turn the waterwheel and drive the Patient Organization.

As you work through the Seven Questions, however, and begin getting to *yes*, you'll feel momentum growing. There are two sides to this lens. As the organization looks through one and tries to answer *yes*, the individual is gazing through the other to do the same. Team members will shoulder most of the burden if they're led rather than managed. Because the organization is granting them more autonomy and working to meet their needs, they won't even see it as a burden—more like a liberating force.

For now, forget about the theory I explored earlier and the more complex pieces of the puzzle. The difficult bits will come in time, and the theory can be skipped entirely if you don't care what's under the hood. Much of my excitement at discovering the Seven Questions had to do with their simplicity. Here are seven basic things every team member and leader can remember and appreciate. Keep it simple.

These are our values. This is our purpose. Can you say yes?

Yes, I Belong.

Yes, I Believe.

Yes, I understand and embrace how I am Accountable.

Yes, I understand and embrace how I am Measured.

Yes, I understand and embrace how I am Heard.

Yes, I understand and embrace how I am Developed.

Yes, I understand and embrace how I am Balanced.

This can be as simple as just having a seasonal conversation with each individual, if you open the door, they will take the lead, power your waterwheel and do the heavy lifting.

Final advice.

If you feel like you have made it complex, you have.

Simplify, Focus, Say No. Be ruthlessly Patient.

Love, Walt

BIBLIOGRAPHY

Adkins, Amy. "Employee Engagement in U.S. Stagnant in 2015." Employee Engagement.

Gallup. January 13, 2016. http://news.gallup.com/poll/188144/employee-engagement-stagnant-2015.aspx.

Chandler, Steve. "Choices for a More Powerful You." http://www.stevechandler.com/choices.html.

Covey, Stephen. *Speed of Trust: The One Thing That Changes Everything.* New York: Simon & Schuster, 2008.

Gallup. "How Millennials Want to Work and Live." 2016. https://enviableworkplace.com/wp-content/uploads/Gallup-How-Millennials-Want-To-Work.pdf.

Gerber, Michael. *The E-Myth: Why Most Businesses Don't Work and What to Do About It.* 2nd ed. Pensacola: Ballinger Publishing, 2004.

Grinnell, John. *Beyond Belief: Awaken Potential, Focus Leadership.* Promethean-Mind Media, 2014.

Harari, Yuval Noah. *Homo Deus: A Brief History of Tomorrow.* New York: Harper Collins, 2017.

Harnish, Verne. *Mastering the Rockefeller Habits: What You Must Do to Increase the Value of Your Growing Firm.* Ashburn: Gazelles Inc., 2002.

———. *Scaling Up: How a Few Companies Make It...and Why the Rest Don't.* Ashburn: Gazelles Inc., 2014.

Lencioni, Patrick. "Make Your Values Mean Something." Harvard Business Review. July 2002. https://hbr.org/2002/07/make-your-values-mean-something.

———. *The Five Dysfunctions of a Team: A Leadership Fable.* Hoboken: Jossey-Bass, 2002.

———. *The Truth About Employee Engagement: A Fable About Addressing the Three Root Causes of Job Misery.* Hoboken: Jossey-Boss, 2015.

Osinga, Frans. *Science, Strategy and War: The Strategic Theory of John Boyd.* Abington: Routledge, 2006.

Re, Daniel E., and Nicholas O. Rule. "Predicting Firm Success From the Facial Appearance of Chief Executive Officers of Non-Profit Organizations." *Perception* 45, no. 10 (October 2016): 1137–1150. https://doi.org/10.1177/0301006616652043.

Rigoni, Brandon, and Bailey Nelson. "Millennials Not Connecting with Their Company's Mission." Business Journal. Gallup. November 15, 2016. http://news.gallup.com/businessjournal/197486/millennials-not-connecting-company-mission.aspx.

———. "Few Millennials Are Engaged at Work." Business Journal. Gallup. August 30, 2016. http://news.gallup.com/businessjournal/195209/few-millennials-engaged-work.aspx.

Robertson, Brian J. *Holacracy: The New Management System for a Rapidly Changing World.* New York: Henry Holt and Company, 2015.

Rock, David. "Managing with the Brain in Mind." strategy+business. August 27, 2009. https://www.strategy-business.com/article/09306?gko=5df7f.

Sinek, Simon. "How great leaders inspire action." Filmed September 2009 at TEDxPuget, Newcastle, WY. Video. 17:58. https://www.ted.com/talks/simon_sinek_how_great_leaders_inspire_action.

Sullivan, Dan. *How the Best Get Better.* Strategic Coach Inc, 2001.

Wickman, Gino. *Traction: Get a Grip on Your Business.* Dallas: BenBella Books, 2012.